I first got to know Lauren after hearing about her accident and discovering she was following me on Twitter. I sent her a tweet, and we have been in touch ever since. Now the tables have turned, and I am the one following Lauren in life . . . a life that is just getting started. Her story teaches us all that there are no accidents in life. Lauren reminds us that God has a master plan for each and every one of us, and hers is to use her voice and her remarkable story to inspire and help others. *Still LoLo* is a beautiful read that helps us remember that sometimes what feels like the end is really just the beginning.

Giuliana Rancic
Anchor, *E! News*

Lauren Scruggs's story is the most inspirational journey I've ever had the opportunity to witness firsthand, and *Still LoLo* truly depicts this young woman's perseverance and faith in the midst of tribulation. I have never seen a family stay so strong and committed to the Lord through such a life-changing event. Lauren's steadfast love of Jesus and her willingness to trust in him with all her heart have done more for her friends and family than she will ever know. Her attitude, joy, and faith are daily reminders of what I aspire to be. I feel blessed to know her.

Tony Romo
Quarterback, Dallas Cowboys

I've personally known the Scruggs family and Lo for ten years. Watching them endure the last year has been tremendous as their faith in Jesus and confidence in his plans for their lives have encouraged and edified my own walk. God often gives stories to strengthen and encourage the weary heart. I think you'll find this story to be one of those.

Matt Chandler
Lead pastor, The Village Church, Dallas
President, Acts 29 Church Planting Network

Our friends, Jeff and Cheryl Scruggs, have a powerful story of God's amazing grace in their broken marriage. But then in a moment their family experienced a shocking calamity—and the story of his remarkable grace continues to be written daily in their lives.

Steve Farrar
Author of *Point Man: How a Man Can Lead His Family*

Mary Farrar
Author of *Choices: For Women Who Long to Discover Life's Best*

still

A spinning propeller,

a horrific accident, and a

family's journey of hope

lauren scruggs

and the Scruggs family

WITH MARCUS BROTHERTON

TYNDALE™
MOMENTUM

An Imprint of
Tyndale House Publishers, Inc.

Visit Tyndale online at www.tyndale.com.

Visit Tyndale Momentum online at www.tyndalemomentum.com.

TYNDALE is a registered trademark of Tyndale House Publishers, Inc. *Tyndale Momentum* and the Tyndale Momentum logo are trademarks of Tyndale House Publishers, Inc. Tyndale Momentum is an imprint of Tyndale House Publishers, Inc.

Still LoLo: A Spinning Propeller, a Horrific Accident, and a Family's Journey of Hope

Designed by Stephen Vosloo

This work is a memoir. Certain names and characteristics have been changed, and some dialogue has been recreated.

Published in association with the literary agency of WordServe Literary Agency, www.wordserveliterary.com.

Library of Congress Cataloging-in-Publication Data

Scruggs, Lauren.
    Still LoLo : a spinning propeller, a horrific accident, and a family's journey of hope / by Lauren Scruggs and the Scruggs family with Marcus Brotherton.
        p. cm.
    ISBN 978-1-4143-7669-1 (hc)
1. Scruggs, Lauren. 2. Aircraft accident victims—Rehabilitation—Texas. 3. Women journalists—Texas—Biography. I. Brotherton, Marcus. II. Title.
    TL553.7.S37 2012
    363.12'4092--dc23
    [B]   2012030266

Printed in the United States of America

18	17	16	15	14	13	12
7	6	5	4	3	2	1

*Thank you so much to each person who has helped
me and my family following the accident.*

Many of you I know, but many of you I don't.

*Words cannot express my level of gratitude for your encouragement,
gifts, prayers, support, and ongoing concern.*

This book is affectionately dedicated to you.

—Love, Lauren

Contents

"Here is the world. Beautiful and terrible things will happen. Don't be afraid."

—FREDERICK BUECHNER

Foreword by Bethany Hamilton

Lauren and I sat comfortably at the nail salon getting our toenails done. Chatting away, we joked about how we should get our fingernails done for half price since we each have only one hand! One of the girls doing our nails asked if we were best friends. We laughed and told her we had just met that day.

I was ecstatic to meet Lauren. We had talked on Skype a few months earlier during a call set up by my nonprofit organization, Friends of Bethany Hamilton, which reaches out to traumatic amputees and shark attack survivors. I made plans to meet up with Lauren during a visit I was making to Texas. Before our visit to the salon, Lauren and I sat over lunch with our moms and talked about our struggles, professional ventures, food, guys, and our faith in Jesus Christ. We talked about anything and everything. We were able to relate on so many levels—first, as fellow followers of Christ, then as sisters in tragedy. It was a blast just getting acquainted!

Having gone through similar experiences, Lauren and I (and our mothers) could really identify with each other. About eight years before, I had been bitten by a shark while surfing and lost my entire left arm. I nearly lost my life as well. Now, after experiencing for myself how God can turn a terrible situation into a great blessing, I sat with Lauren. Just six months earlier she had suffered the loss of her left hand and eye. Yet the God-given joy and strength that comes from trusting him whole-heartedly emanated from her radiant smile.

Since the day we met, I've had a chance to read *Still LoLo*. It brought me through so many familiar emotions. I smiled, laughed, and cried as I read about what Lauren has encountered. Life often feels like a long, arduous climb, and I felt much of that pain as I read all that Lauren went through—from her parents' struggles during her early childhood, to her challenges as a young woman trying to find her way in this world, to the night she lost her arm and almost lost her life.

I read with compassion about the struggles Lauren faced through all of these life-changing events. Yet in the face of so many overwhelming obstacles, Lauren, her parents, and her twin sister, Brittany, found their source of strength and hope in Jesus Christ—in much the same way that my family and I did.

The members of Lauren's family each give their own perspective in *Still LoLo*, so they tell their story *together*. It's a beautiful way to share the many struggles and triumphs this family has experienced. You'll see how God mended and healed each of their hearts again and again. You'll discover how he brought about unity and restoration through each difficulty they faced.

You'll cheer as you read how Lauren's determination and her family's love sustained her after her life-threatening accident. One of my favorite stories in the book tells about the time, just days after her accident, when Lauren deliberately took thirty steps after her physical therapist asked if she might be able to walk twenty. Because of Lauren's story, I have been freshly renewed, inspired, and motivated to take those extra "ten steps" in my own life. She is a beautiful ray of sunshine, and I am glad to have her as a friend.

As I read *Still LoLo*, I was brought back to that day I sat in the nail salon with Lauren. We looked like childhood friends as we shared our stories. I know I was encouraged by the hope that my new dear friend told me she was discovering on her journey through life.

As you venture into *Still LoLo* and learn more about Lauren's attitude toward life, I hope you will gain the strength and motivation, as I have, to keep pressing on—no matter what struggles come your way. May you learn to live by Lauren's definition of everyday courage: "Even when life hits you hard, keep on going."

I look forward to watching LoLo succeed in life and hope to join her in some of her future endeavors.

Join this family on their journey, and be encouraged!

Aloha,

Bethany Hamilton
Author of *Soul Surfer: A True Story of Faith, Family, and Fighting to Get Back on the Board*

Overture

Lauren

The old man didn't look like an angel, but years later I wondered if he was one.

He was sitting on a bench outside a sporting goods store in Plano, Texas, with his legs crossed casually. As he leaned back and looked into the sky, I noticed that his pants were tattered. A stain from a pen blotched the bottom of his shirt pocket. Near his side lay a clear, plastic ziplock bag. I didn't want to be nosy and stare too long at the bag, but inside it I could see a pair of men's underwear, a toothbrush, and the folded corner of an extra shirt. It was a beautiful day in 2002, not too hot, with a denim-blue sky and feathery clouds. I was fifteen.

"It's . . . Joshua, isn't it?" asked my dad hesitantly as we walked toward the bench and paused. "Joshua—right? Is that you?"

"Yes. I recognize you as well, my friend. I was a visitor in your Sunday school class at church last week." The man's words sounded too crisp to originate from Texas. He spoke with a lilt, not a drawl, like maybe years ago he'd lived in Kenya or Uganda.

"Yeah, I thought I recognized you from church," said my dad. It was just the two of us on the way to the store. My twin sister, Brittany, and my mom were back at our house. "You waiting for somebody?" Dad's voice was friendly, not accusing.

"Oh. No, my friend. I am just enjoying the day."

Out of the corner of my eye, I noticed my dad look closely at the man. "You live around here?"

"No, not here," the man said slowly, as if choosing the right words. "I live over there. Down by the bridge."

Dad winced. "Joshua, can I ask . . . have you eaten today?"

Joshua shook his head.

Dad nodded. "Then why don't you come have dinner with us."

I tucked a strand of blonde hair behind my ear and stayed quiet, letting Dad do all the talking. Several times Brittany and I had gone with Dad down to the projects in South Dallas to help out with an inner-city ministry, but inviting homeless people back to our house wasn't anything we'd ever done before. We were the quintessential Texas suburban family. Two cars. Cowboys fans. There wasn't an actual white picket fence around our yard, but there may as well have been. I thought it was cool for Dad to invite a homeless man to dinner, but I also felt a twinge of uneasiness. We were stepping into unknown territory, and I had no idea what would come next.

Joshua's eyes brightened. "I would be very grateful for a meal. As long as it is okay with your wife."

"Let me call Cheryl." Dad flipped open his phone and hit speed dial. "I'm sure she won't mind."

I need to explain that it wasn't out of the ordinary for Dad to talk to people he barely knew. He's a real people person. But it *was* out of the ordinary for him to single out and remember a visitor from his Sunday school class. It wasn't exactly a small gathering where you'd instantly notice someone new. This was a Dallas-sized Sunday school that several hundred people attended each week. It was more like a church-within-a-church, a large group where a lot of people came and went.

Joshua came home with us that night. We all just hung around the table in our kitchen, talking quickly and easily with Joshua like he was an old friend. He spoke easily, eloquently, almost regally.

But there was something strange about him too. He ate our salad, pot roast, and potatoes. He drank our sweet tea and said thanks. But he asked extensive questions about the food we ate, how it was prepared and where it came from, and he was careful to not let his meat touch his vegetables, almost like he had a prescribed way of living, a habit tied to another culture. After dinner was over, he asked to use our shower. Mom fidgeted in her chair, but Dad said yes right away and got up to show him where it was. After Joshua was situated, Dad took some toothpaste and deodorant and extra clothes to him.

A special meeting was being held at our church that night. I think it was a missions report. Mom and Dad took Joshua with them to the meeting while Brittany and I stayed home and did homework. When they came back, it was time for bed. Mom glanced at Dad, and Dad shrugged, got a blanket and clean sheets out of the closet, and showed Joshua to the guest room.

I didn't know what to think of this homeless man sleeping in our house. He wasn't tall or broad-shouldered, like Dad is, and he hadn't showed any sign of being violent or anything. Secretly I wondered if he carried a knife, but even if he did, I knew Dad would protect us. In the morning Dad was leaving on a business trip for two days, and I didn't know what would happen to the homeless man then. The whole night, things felt unpredictable.

The next morning, Joshua ate breakfast with us. He asked a lot of questions about the fruit and pancakes, and he drank orange juice, not coffee. Dad was going to take him to a hotel, and when Dad got back from his business trip he promised to drive him over to the neighboring town of McKinney. There was a homeless shelter there called The Samaritan Inn that I knew helped people get back on their feet.

We hugged Joshua and said our good-byes. Dad drove him to the hotel and headed out on his trip, and it was just Mom, Brittany, and me in the house alone. I think I was brushing my teeth, getting ready for school, when I heard Brittany call from the guest room where she'd been taking the sheets off the bed. "Mom! I think you're going to want to see this." There was a tremor in her voice. I heard Mom's footsteps pound down the hallway. I was right behind her. Brittany's eyes were round. She passed the envelope to Mom.

Inside was a handwritten letter from Joshua. Tiny, perfect, single-spaced writing. I counted seven pages. After Mom read each page, she handed it to me. I gasped. Joshua had described our family to a tee, then written beyond what could be seen at the present time. That was the shocking part. His writing was laced with Scripture, and it was like he was seeing a clear image of us in a mirror where we could see only the reflection dimly. I'd compare his letter to a lengthy inscription in a high school yearbook, a prediction about our next years, about things still to come. Maybe he had experienced a feeling he hadn't felt in a while, the warmth and closeness of a family, and he simply needed to express what he felt on paper.

"Your two daughters were angels to me in action and words," he began, and there was a lot of kind description after that of every member of our family. For page after page, this homeless man wrote with the confident authority of a biblical prophet. I imagined him wearing camel skins for clothes and eating locusts and wild honey.

Specific to my sister, he wrote, "Brittany is the salt of the family. She will live a life of kindness with attainment of a man who will bring her to the top of the goal. Journey will be an avenue of success. And there will be an abundance of good luck in the family she will build."

About me, he wrote, "Her sister will be a warrior. She will always win battles and bring good news and things of highest qualities. She will be aligned with VIPs. Her aptitude, love of family, and nature will be graced by the eminent people of the world. She will be a great traveler. Her words will penetrate the hearts of great men and women. She will bathe in the company of good friends. She is an inventor . . . and she will swim into this arena in another form of leadership."

I didn't know what to make of it. I didn't know any eminent people. And I certainly didn't feel like a warrior.

How could this mysterious homeless man know anything about me? It didn't make sense. But the gist of what he wrote burrowed into my soul and lodged there. He was predicting that life was going to hold out something vast to me, that God had something big planned for my future. It would involve innovation and travel and writing and celebrities and a battle larger than I could have ever expected.

I felt excited but also apprehensive. I didn't know if any of the homeless man's predictions would come true. But if they did, it sounded like whatever was coming—good or bad—would soon arrive with unstoppable force.

CHAPTER 1

An Unmistakable Premonition

Lauren

Dad looked like a ghost.

Not one of those screechy phantoms you see in a horror movie, but like a pale version of his usually cheery self—white as a sheet, except for the dark circles under his eyes.

"Cheryl." His voice was thin. He coughed, then said, "I don't know if I can do this tonight after all."

"You want us to take you home?" Mom said. "We're not very far."

Dad was behind the wheel, but he nodded at Mom's offer, coughed again, and turned the car toward home. Beads of sweat lay across his forehead.

It was Saturday, December 3, 2011, about 4 p.m.

From our house in West Plano, we were on our way to another suburb of Dallas called Flower Mound. We were heading to The Village Church, where we normally attend, for a regular weekend service. Advent season was upon us, and it felt like Christmas was in the air. From the backseat, I reached over and gave my dad a warm pat on his shoulder. "Have some chicken soup," I said. "Maybe a little oil of oregano mixed with orange juice. Fights infections, you know. I think there's some in the kitchen pantry."

Dad coughed again and grinned weakly.

I wasn't in the habit of babying my parents, especially not my dad. But there were definitely days I felt like a grown-up around them, a colleague more than a kid. At age twenty-three, I wasn't a child anymore. True enough, I had recently moved back home to start my online fashion journal, *LOLO Magazine*. But living at home was just temporary. I'd graduated from college with academic honors. I'd successfully completed two internships in New York City, where I'd lived on my own. I'd traveled to Paris, Montreal, and New York to report on their Fashion Weeks, the intensive seven-day stretch where all the next season's new designs are showcased. I'd done numerous video-reporting segments where I'd interviewed actors, celebrities, and fashion industry insiders. Nearly nine years had passed since the homeless man's prediction of a big life and a big battle for me. Life felt big some days, but nothing that could be considered huge. At least, not yet.

The only reason I had moved home was that Mom and Dad were being gracious, giving me free room and board for a season or two until my magazine began to pay for itself. I spent every waking minute on *LOLO Magazine*. Most days I'd start at eight in the morning and go hard until midnight. The staff consisted of me and Shannon Yoachum, another young, entrepreneurial journalist who lived just a few hours away in Austin. We were throwing our hearts into the project. Our personal tagline was "Live Out Loud," and that's how we approached our work—with the volume turned all the way up. Shannon and I had been close friends since kindergarten, and these days we were writing and editing columns, contacting press agents for photographs, interviewing designers, connecting with industry insiders, and soliciting articles from freelancers. The magazine had been going only a few months, but already we were getting many thousands of hits per month, and at least that many on a separate fashion blog that I wrote.

We dropped Dad back at home so he could lie down and fight his cold, and Mom and I headed to church by ourselves. I love hanging out with just my mom. She's one of the most intelligent, caring women I know. She and my dad both work as marriage counselors. They travel all over the country sharing their story, and they've written a book that helps a lot of couples have better, stronger relationships.

We got to church early and saved seats for friends of my parents, Mike and Shannon, along with three friends of theirs. The plan was for all of us to head over to Mike and Shannon's house after church for a chili feast. I've babysat Mike and Shannon's daughter plenty of times and tutored her with her homework, and I house-sit for them when they're out of town. I'm like one of the family over there.

Everybody arrived at church, and the band cranked up. We all stood for a time of worship and sang along. Then Paul David Tripp, a guest speaker that night, took the stage.

"I don't know if you've thought about this or not," he began, "but you're hardwired for hope. You don't live by instinct. Every decision you make, every choice you make, every response you have to the situations and relationships of your life is fueled by and motivated by hope. Your story, the story of your life, is a hope story. Your happiest moments are hope moments. Your saddest moments are about hope dashed, hope destroyed. You're always looking for hope. You're always attaching the hope of your heart to something."[1]

I had no inkling yet of the journey of hope I would soon embark on, but I could relate to what Paul said. Already I hoped for a lot. I wanted my magazine to be a huge success. But it wasn't just about numbers. I hoped my magazine would help people live better lives. Sure, it's about fashion, about looking good and feeling good. But it's also about being confident, expressing who you truly are. It's about going places and doing things that matter.

I also hoped for that special someone. I guess everybody my age does. Only a month before, I'd broken up with my boyfriend, James. It felt like the right decision at the time. James is six feet tall and has dark brown hair. He's in good shape, and plenty of girls would line up to date him. He's one of those sincere, solid guys who's always there for you, always says the right thing.

But . . . ah, what was it exactly? In the back of my mind roamed an image of another guy. He was only a figment of my imagination, an ideal whose existence I pondered. I could picture him—the ultimate boyfriend—tall; beachy good looks; laid-back yet driven personality; tender and caring; funny and genuine; a heart for God; and a clear direction in life. But I needed to be honest with myself. This was real life, and James was everything a girl could ever ask for. Almost, anyway. But this other guy—this idealized image of the perfect mate—well, maybe he was worth holding out for, at least a little while longer. Or maybe he was just a dangerous fantasy, like a glossy picture in a magazine.

James handled the breakup in a totally good way. We reassured each other we'd stay friends. We always did. We'd actually broken up once before and then gotten back together. "Promise me you'll be really careful, Lo," he said when he dropped me off at my house the night we broke up. "I can't quite explain it, but I have this feeling like something bad is coming your way."

I nodded, and we hugged, even as I shivered a little. James had always been there for me. He saw God's purpose in things, even difficult things. What more could a girl ever want?

XO

When church was over, we headed to Mike and Shannon's house in McKinney, which is about twenty minutes from our house. Sometimes it's hard for someone who's not from Texas to understand the size of things in this state. For instance, if you go to a restaurant and order a soft drink, they don't have small, medium, and large. They have small, medium, and "Texas-size." People just do things in a big way around here.

Mike and Shannon are no exceptions. Everything Mike does, he does in a Texas-size way. Mike buys and sells companies, in addition to being a real estate developer. Their home is one of about 130 houses built around a private airstrip. One of Mike's hobbies is flying, and he owns three planes.

We all ate chili and salad around the long wooden table in Mike and Shannon's dining room. Some other friends came over. There were maybe a dozen people total. Christmas music floated in from the sound system. Everybody was just talking and laughing. Nobody was drinking that I remember. It wasn't that type of party.

"Hey, Mike, you mind if I borrow your plane?" one of Mike's friends asked.

"Help yourself," Mike said. "You know what to do." Mike and his friend, I knew, both had their pilot's licenses.

"Who wants to go flying?" the friend asked. "The Christmas lights are going to be great tonight." A bunch of people waved their hands.

I don't know how or why I got to go for a ride first. Everyone else must have been feeling generous. So I followed Mike's friend out through the backyard and into the hangar that's directly behind Mike's house. Another friend, also a licensed pilot, came along to help me board the plane. On the far end of the hangar is a huge garage door for the planes, and beyond that lies a tarmac area. Then there's a taxiway, and beyond that a runway. It's like a house built around a golf course, except Mike's house is built around an airstrip.

With the guys' help, I climbed over the plane's stabilizer bar and slid into the seat behind the pilot. It was a small plane with only two seats. We put on headphones so we could talk to each other once we were in the air. The pilot went through his checklist, started the plane and warmed it up, and we taxied out.

The night was dark and rainy. Shadowy clouds were thick above us in a starless sky. For some reason I began to feel cold. The heater was on in the tiny plane, but what I felt wasn't that type of cold. It was more of a tingle. A shiver. I took a deep breath and looked out the window.

"Nice lights," the pilot said.

"Uh-huh."

The feeling shot up my spine again. Unmistakable fear. *This is stupid*, I thought. *Completely stupid.* Not the experience of flying but this definite feeling of dread coursing through my body. Mike had vouched for his friend as a strong pilot who was qualified on several levels and owned his own plane. *Get a grip, Lo*, I told myself. *You need to relax.*

Up in the air, the atmosphere grew calmer. The rain let up and turned into a slight mist. It might have even stopped. There was no thunder or lightning. No strong winds. All I heard was the friendly drone of the plane's engine and the occasional crackle over the microphone's earpiece. But I still couldn't shake this crazy fear.

I couldn't shake it at all.

My body grew tense, and my breathing became shallow. My heart thumped in my chest. It wasn't like me to be afraid. Certainly not in situations like this. I'm the type of girl who loves an adventure, particularly a tame adventure like we were having tonight. I like to ride bikes and go snow skiing and slalom waterskiing. In my bedroom is a very cool street longboard with a Hawaiian sunset motif that I've ridden for years. Even when Brittany and I were five-year-old kids and Dad took us skiing at Vail, my sister would ease down the bunny slopes while I'd bounce through black diamond moguls. So why was I so afraid of this flight? I gripped both sides of the plane's seat even tighter. And then it hit me. *We're going to crash.* I thought my heart was going to explode. *Jesus,* I prayed. *This plane's going down, and we're both going to die. I just know it. Oh Lord, my parents and sister. Please watch over them. Jesus, Jesus. Whatever happens, God, my life is in your hands.*

I'm sure the Christmas lights were pretty that night, but I was too nervous to really concentrate on them. I don't remember anything in particular. No landmarks. No huge display at a shopping center. Just darkness and lights and the fields and streets around McKinney. The plane flew in a big circle.

And then we landed.

The air went out of me like a rush from a leaky tire. My fear went along with it. We were safe. Completely safe. The plane taxied back to Mike's house and pulled up facing into the wind and parked on the tarmac, all set for whoever was going to fly next. *Hmmm, maybe I'm cracking up,* I thought. *I wonder what that was all about?*

I don't remember the pilot saying anything directly to me. I don't remember anything he said at all. He might have said something. I just don't remember. It was hard to hear him without my speaker on. It's still pretty loud with the plane's engine running, sitting on the tarmac.

I remember sliding out of the plane.

I remember my feet touching the tarmac.

I remember the sky was black; I was on the dark side of the plane.

Those three memories took place in a split second, about the time it takes to walk two steps.

It was December 3, 2011, and after that split second, I remember absolutely nothing.

CHAPTER 2

Horror

Cheryl (Lauren's mom)

Shannon was screaming.

I looked up from my coffee inside Mike and Shannon's house where I was sitting with another couple after dinner.

Screaming. Screaming.

I set down my coffee cup and stood for a moment, stunned. What was Shannon saying? "I think she lost her left hand. It's Lauren! Lauren!" Shannon was running toward me.

Instantly my mind connected with my feet. I sprinted outside through the airplane hangar and onto the tarmac on the other side. In the inky darkness I saw the plane. The propeller still swinging. Lauren on the tarmac, lying crumpled on her face, her left arm underneath her body. I couldn't see any of her arm or hand. Mike was already crouched next to her. Lauren wasn't moving. A pool of blood spread out beneath her like a red mud puddle. She looked lifeless. I prayed on reflex while running to Lauren, flung myself down next to her, and put my hand on her shoulder. "Lauren, it's Mom. Can you hear me?"

Lauren groaned and started to move. I put my hand on her forehead to brush away her hair. When I pulled my hand away, it was covered in blood. Lauren groaned again. She was trying to get up, but Mike was holding her down. "Stay down, Lauren," he was murmuring. "Help's right around the corner. Don't move, baby. Don't move." Lauren writhed and then lay still before trying to move again. I had no idea how to help her. The night swirled and grew fuzzy. I could hear voices around me. Footsteps. People running. I began to tremble, feeling like I might pass out. I kept praying, praying, praying. Shock overtook my body as snatches from a phone call to 911 ran through my ears.

> SHANNON: A girl walked into an airplane prop. I need an ambulance immediately.
> DISPATCHER: Where are you at, ma'am? [The dispatcher pressed for details.] Was it moving when it happened?
> SHANNON: Yes. I think it cut her hand off.

Out of the corner of my eye, I saw Shannon handing the phone to someone else, who explained to the 911 operator that Lauren was somewhat responsive, and that there was a lot of blood, but it wasn't clear where it was coming from.

> DISPATCHER: Is she conscious?
> MAN: Yes.

Shannon came over to me and crouched low. Lauren's moans were growing louder. I kept praying.

> MAN: Do you want me to let her turn over?
> DISPATCHER: Is she trying to?
> MAN: She's trying to, yes.
> DISPATCHER: Okay, we don't want to hurt her any further than she already is.
> MAN: I agree.

I glanced at my watch. 8:54 p.m. Right around the corner from Mike's house is a fire station. A fire truck raced down the side road near the house and pulled up near the tarmac. It had been only minutes since the accident. Five minutes, maybe six. An ambulance arrived at nearly the same time. A minute went by. Another. Lauren's moans turned into wails. Over my head I heard a helicopter. The CareFlite crew, air medical transport, was there in a heartbeat. Paramedics were at my shoulder. "You guys need to step aside," they said. Voices were terse. Mike took my arm and led me off the tarmac and into the hangar. We could hear everything through the open doors. Lauren was screaming now, screaming in pain. Mike was trying to distract me. Horrific screams. Chilling screams. Even the paramedics looked shaken. As they worked on Lauren, they were praying out loud.

"It's good she's conscious," Mike said to me. His voice was low. "They've asked her if she knows her name and if she knows where she is. She just said 'Lauren Scruggs' and 'at an airport.'"

A thousand gallons of adrenaline coursed through my body. I felt helpless. Powerless. All I could do was stand in the hangar and keep out of the way. In my mind flashed an image of Lauren at two years old. She was riding one of those rolling toy horses around the back patio when she hit a bump, tumbled off, and hit her chin on the concrete. There were no stitches required, nothing like that. Just a bump and a bruise, and I was able to gather her in my arms like any good mother would do and kiss away the hurt. How I longed to be able to do that now.

"They're going to take her to either Parkland or Baylor," Mike said. "They'll let us know once they're in the air."

"I want to go with her. I need to be with my daughter."

"They won't let you be in the helicopter," Mike said. "It's going to be okay. They need to put all their attention on Lauren right now. We'll follow in the car." The night was sprinkling with rain. Misty. Wet. Shannon ran and got me a jacket from inside the house. I was shaking uncontrollably.

They were lifting Lauren onto the stretcher. "Why is my hand white?" Lauren asked loudly through screams. "I can't see it! I can't see!" Her shirt was over her hand.

I wanted to run to Lauren, but Mike held me back. I kept praying. The paramedics raced the gurney to the helicopter and packed Lauren inside.

"They should be leaving by now," Mike said out of the corner of his mouth, almost like he didn't want me to hear. "Why isn't the helicopter leaving? It should be taking off by now."

A paramedic was walking around the tarmac, a flashlight in his hand. Another was walking by the grass at the edge of the taxiway. He also had a flashlight.

Still, the helicopter sat, its blades circling.

The first paramedic came into the open hangar and looked underneath something. He was at least forty feet from the crash site. He glanced toward Mike.

"Can I help you?" Mike called out. His voice rose at the end, clearly perturbed.

The paramedic put his one finger to his mouth for Mike to be silent and looked at me, almost like a nudge. I took the cue and looked away. The paramedic didn't want me to see.

He had found her hand.

CHAPTER 3

Racing to the Hospital

Jeff (Lauren's dad)

One moment I was sitting in my easy chair at home watching TV.

The next moment I was on my knees.

In between the two moments, the call came from Mike's wife, Shannon. Her voice sounded garbled, erratic. I couldn't make out details, although I grasped enough. My daughter had been seriously injured in an accident with a plane's propeller, and they were racing her to Baylor Medical Center. Whether she would live or die was unknown.

Maybe it was the cold medicine I'd taken half an hour earlier. I don't know. But when I hung up the phone, I heard a sharp wailing sound in the house. It ricocheted off walls and pierced my heart like a lance. *Who's wailing?* I thought. Then I realized—it was me.

In the next moment I was standing in the kitchen. A minute later I was in the bathroom, my face perched over the toilet. I was walking down the hallway. I was walking out to the garage. Pacing. Pacing. Trying to figure out what to do next. Crying. Praying. Pacing. Pacing. Calling out to God, "Oh Lord, save my daughter!" *Slow down, Jeff,*

I thought. *Get a grip. Call someone. You don't want to be alone right now. You're in no shape to drive.*

I called my good friend Chris Crawford. He's a dermatologist, and he and his wife, Dana, are like a brother and sister to Cheryl and me. Chris and Dana were out at a restaurant in North Dallas along with their daughter, Candice, who's just a bit older than Lauren. I found out later that they thought I was calling to invite them over to our house after dinner, like we often do. They had just ordered appetizers and blackened fish, one of our favorite meals. "Heeeey! What's going on?" Chris answered the phone in his usual friendly voice.

There was a pause.

Again came that strange, horrible sound. Where was it coming from? Bouncing off my walls like that. Again, I realized the wail came from me.

"Jeff? Where are you! What's wrong? Are you hurt?"

I managed to choke out a single word, "No." But I couldn't get any further. I tried to say, "Lauren's been in an accident" and "propeller" and "please come over right now," but I don't know what actually jumbled out of my mouth. All I heard was Chris saying, "Don't move, Jeff. I'll be right there."

I kept pacing, praying, wailing. I called another close friend, Chris Wilson. He's one of my workout partners and strong as an ox, exactly the kind of friend you need in times of crisis. His phone went straight to voice mail. When it beeped, I yelled, "Where are you?! Why aren't you answering? Lauren's been in an accident. It's bad. Really, really bad."

I hung up and paced some more. Chris Wilson called me straight back. "It ain't like you to yell, brother. I'll be right over."

I called my other daughter, Brittany. She and her husband, Shaun, were downtown enjoying a performance of *The Nutcracker*, and I knew their phones wouldn't be turned on in the auditorium.

"Dad, is that you?" Shaun said. The dull roar of a crowd could be heard. "It's intermission. I just this moment switched on my phone. Why are you yelling?"

Dead air. The call dropped. I dialed again. This time Brittany answered.

"Dad, slow down. You're not making any sense. Here—I'm going to hand the phone back to Shaun."

I said something about an airplane and a propeller and that they'd taken Lauren to the hospital.

"We'll meet you there right away," Shaun said.

Chris Crawford and Chris Wilson both pulled into my driveway at the same time. I had no idea how Chris Crawford had made it from downtown Dallas to Plano that quickly. Doors slammed. Both men ran up the front steps and burst inside. There was no need to knock.

"They're taking her to Baylor," I said. I already had my coat on. "Let's go."

"Dude, you look pale," Chris Wilson said. "You go with the doctor. I'll follow in my car."

Chris Crawford loaded me in his sedan and turned the key. The engine started with a deep growl. He screeched the tires and accelerated like a dragster. Everything became a blur. We raced along side streets and merged on the Dallas North Tollway, heading for downtown. Traffic was light, and I saw the speedometer inch past 110 mph.

Reality came and went. Sometimes I was wailing. Sometimes I was silent. Chris was praying out loud. Sometimes I was praying at the same time, all in a rush. "Oh God, oh God, oh God, how could this have happened?" Then I was in and out some more. Rocking in my seat. Back and forth. Back and forth. Waves of nausea. Maybe I was back at home again, watching TV with a bad head cold. No, this was real. I was in the front seat of Chris's car, and we were speeding down the toll road to the hospital. I lost sight of Chris Wilson's car behind us. I think he was keeping his speed down to a cool 85.

"Jeff, talk to me here." Chris's voice shifted to a doctor's clinical tone. "Did Shannon give any details? Do you have any indication of how serious the accident was?"

"No, not really." I was still trying to piece everything together in my head. "Shannon just said something about her hand."

"Did the propeller hit Lauren in the head or face too?"

"The propeller hit her head. That's all she said that I can remember—and that it was bad."

I knew what Chris was thinking. Doctors always imagine the worst. They're around death and dying too much. Even dermatologists. His mind was churning. He was calculating a hit to the head by an airplane propeller, and he was doing the math. Start with a powerful engine. Factor in a couple thousand rpms. Apply to soft tissue, brain material, bone, skin. He was picturing textbook images of trauma injuries he had seen. A hand sliced off by a lawn mower blade. An arm caught in a farm cultivator. Chris sensed the gravity of the situation. He just wasn't articulating it to me. Lauren wasn't going to survive an accident like this. We were going to screech to a stop at the hospital, and the surgeons were going to come out and say, "Sorry, she didn't make it. There wasn't anything we could do."

"I think I'm going to be sick," I said and slid down in my seat.

Chris checked the rearview mirror and veered to a side lane. "Okay, we can stop."

"No!" I righted myself. "We've got to get to the hospital!"

Chris began to pray out loud again, slipping on his doctor's hat, even in prayer. "Jesus, Lord God. You gotta help them stabilize her, get her blood pressure up. It can't be the carotid artery, Lord. You gotta pull her through."

I was navigating mental and emotional waves. It almost became a pattern. I was okay for a while and then not. I wailed for a while and then was silent. I talked, spilling in a rush whatever came to mind—"I knew something bad was going to happen with that flying. I never did feel comfortable with that. Why wasn't I there? I could have done something." And then I was crying out to the Lord, "God, please save my daughter's life."

Another call came through. The helicopter's flight had been diverted. They were taking Lauren to Parkland Memorial Hospital, not Baylor. Chris changed lanes again, and for the first time that evening I saw him smile faintly. "Thank goodness it's Parkland," he said. "That's an awesome place to be in this town if you get a serious injury. She'll stand the best chance there."

We cut off the toll road, rounded the corner onto Harry Hines Boulevard, and screeched into the hospital's parking lot. As we jumped out, we heard the helicopter flying in and landing. Identical timing. God must have orchestrated that event perfectly. It felt good that we were there. At least now Lauren would have family in the same building with her.

Outside Parkland it was crowded, as it always is, and a policeman stood at the front door, ushering people in and out. Chris and I walked through the glass doors and told the guy at the counter who we were. He pointed us to the ER's waiting room. Parkland is the county hospital; everyone goes there. A sign near the entrance reads, "Founded in 1894."

The chairs in the waiting room were cold and cushionless, made out of hard meshed metal. They'd been all red once, but the paint was flaking. Sitting on one of those chairs in the ER felt like sitting on a tombstone. People were all around me, but I couldn't hear what anybody was saying. Chris stuck to my side.

For a while we were by ourselves. A chaplain came by and introduced herself. "I'm going to be your facilitator," she said. "I know Lauren's here. And I know she's alive." Then we prayed together.

It might have been only ten minutes later when Cheryl arrived along with Shannon. They had farther to come than we did. My wife and I hadn't talked yet. Shannon had relayed all the information to me over the phone. As soon as Cheryl saw us, she started crying. We ran to each other and wrapped our arms around each other, both sobbing. "We were there," she said. "I saw it." Cheryl's shirt was covered in blood.

I tried to pull myself together for my wife's sake. I gathered some composure. People began to show up. Friends of ours. People we knew from church. Steve and Mary Farrar. Matt Chandler, our pastor. Chris's wife, Dana, and their daughter, Candice. The chaplain showed us to a smaller, more private waiting area. More friends showed up. Still more. Shaun and Brittany arrived along with Chris Wilson—they'd all pulled into the parking lot at the same time and came in together. We were jammed into the tiny room. Hospital personnel showed us to a window-less conference room down the hallway. It had some tables in it. We were thankful for the space. More friends showed up. Still more. The room loaded up. Seventy-five, eighty people, maybe closer to a hundred.

"People, the magic word is *stabilized*," Chris Crawford said. "Pray we'll hear that—and hear it soon. That's the news that will change everything. Let's pray we hear this word before the night is over." The room filled with prayer.

As the clock ticked, no magic word came. It felt like a nightmare. *This can't be happening*, I thought. I was sitting, sometimes lying, on the floor, rocking back and forth, back and forth. We had lost all composure again. Cheryl, who was sobbing, was sitting in a chair but kept throwing her back up, lurching erratically. Dana was with her, rubbing her back, keeping her close.

Just before midnight a doctor came in and cleared his throat. "I need to speak to the parents." His face was tense.

Instantly the room quieted down.

"Whatever needs to be said, you can say it to everybody here," I said. "We're all family."

"All eighty of you?" He raised an eyebrow.

I nodded.

"Lauren's condition has stabilized," he said. The magic word. Eighty people breathed a collective sigh of relief. The tension scaled back instantly. I thought I even heard a cheer. "Heart rate's good. Blood pressure's good. Breathing's good. She's not going to die," the doctor added. "But there's still a lot of work to be done. She'll be in surgery most of the night. Before she goes under, the immediate family can have five minutes with her."

Cheryl caught my eye, and I nodded. We got up and followed the doctor down the hallway to a small trauma room off the ER. Brittany, Shaun, and Chris Crawford came with us. The walls in the hallway were scuffed from endless bumps with metal carts and gurneys. We walked into the room.

I noticed Lauren's lips first.

Her face was swollen; they'd pumped so many fluids into her. Underneath her chin was a white, plastic neck collar that framed the underside of her face in a V. It looked like a picture frame highlighting the bottom of her mouth. Her lips were closed, and the left side of her mouth was pulled back slightly. Lauren was neither smiling nor frowning. She was just there. Yet her lips were perfect. Untouched. The same as ever. That's what I noticed.

A pile of gray, red, and green cords and tubes cascaded around her. Half of her head was shaved, and one eye was covered. A thick white bandage was wrapped around her left shoulder. Over the sheet, I could just see her right hand. It had cuts and bruises on it from where she'd hit the pavement. Her left arm was completely covered. Heart monitors and machines I didn't recognize ringed the bed. A red light to one side blinked on and off, on and off.

"All things considered, she looks great," Chris said. He was trying to give us a medical perspective. We knew things could have been a lot worse. Lauren still had a face. She could have been missing huge chunks of skin or scalp, like divots that get ripped up at a golf course.

I didn't touch her for fear of passing on the germs from my cold. But I wanted to hold her. To tell her everything was going to be all right. To whisper into her ear the songs I used to sing when she was a little girl.

Cheryl bent down and kissed the side of Lauren's face. "It's Mom," Cheryl whispered. "I'm here, and it's going to be okay." Cheryl had grown completely calm. I knew she was speaking for both of us with a strength that came from far above.

Everything was completely quiet in the room. There was no response from Lauren. Whatever battle we were fighting had just begun.

CHAPTER 4

Life Unexpected

Cheryl

As we walked back through the hallway from Lauren's trauma room to our group's waiting area, I noticed something different. The walls of Parkland were still the same dingy white, with an occasional block painted a flat green. The same smell of hospital disinfectant saturated the air. The floor still looked both polished and scuffed at the same time. What was different now was that, for the first time in hours, I was breathing normally.

My watch read just after midnight, Sunday, December 4, 2011. These were the first minutes of the first full day after Lauren's accident. Jeff took my hand in his and pulled me close as we walked so our shoulders touched. We were going to make it through this. All of us— Lauren especially, as well as everybody who loved her so deeply. That's what felt different. Somehow we were all going to be all right. And that undergirding of friendship was what kept me going. *We.* We were all in this together. We weren't alone.

Back in the waiting area, Chris Crawford filled in the larger group of people on how Lauren looked and what he thought the possible prognoses for recovery would be. Multiple teams of surgeons would be operating on Lauren throughout the night. One team for the brain. Another for the eye. Hand. Face. Shoulder. We weren't sure yet of all the operations scheduled. Each time another surgery was begun, a new team would take over.

A hospital administrator came in with a clipboard and asked Jeff and me to fill out some paperwork, forms, waivers—I wasn't quite sure what. We scribbled our signatures and sat awhile. Then another administrator came in with more paperwork. Again we scribbled on page after page, barely conscious of what we were signing. We sat some more. Paced some more. Then another administrator came in, and we signed another notebook full of paperwork. It felt like we were buying a house.

The clock ticked to 1 a.m., 2 a.m., 3 a.m. A few people left to go home and catch some sleep, but most stayed. Pockets of friends gathered in small groups and kept praying. Waiting. Our church's music pastor, Michael Bleecker, quietly sang some worship songs. More praying. More waiting.

Poor Jeff. He had been feeling miserable with his cold even before the accident. As the night wore on, I seemed to be gaining strength, gaining confidence, thinking with a clearer head. But Jeff was going the other direction. For a while he tried to sleep, curled up on a coat on the floor. Then he paced. Then he sat with his head in his hands. Then he cried.

Hour after hour Chris Crawford and Chris Wilson sat next to my husband. They talked with him. Prayed with him. Let him cough on them. I knew that as much as Jeff needed me as his wife right now, he needed his buddies just as much, maybe even more. For years they had honed their friendship like iron sharpens iron. Now they were slashing through the anguish of this night together. Brothers in battle. Soldiers at war.

My mind drifted. Waiting rooms can prompt that response in a person. I prayed. I waited. I talked with people in the room. But I also had large moments of empty space when my mind ran free. Maybe time sped up in my head, because flashes of Lauren's life came to me. Snippets of conversation. Images of years past. Funny memories of things she'd said or done.

I thought about how miraculous it was that Lauren had ever been born in the first place. God had a purpose for her life; I'd known it even before she was born. And now as a young adult, Lauren had only begun to step into that purpose. God knew every move my daughter made, and he had set into motion every one of her days. He would keep her alive until the purpose for her life was accomplished. Lauren would heal. I knew it for a fact. I knew it by faith.

XO

How strange were the circumstances that led up to Lauren being conceived. Years ago the odds had been stacked against her birth. I was all set to marry someone else. Back in 1981, I was in my early twenties, finishing up college at Memphis State and seriously dating a guy named Bill. Evenings, I worked at an upscale restaurant to put myself through school. One night a tall, hunky stranger came in and sat in my section. After ordering, he asked me out on a date. There was no way I would say yes. Bill worked in the same restaurant, just a few bus stations away. I smiled and declined the offer, but inside I was definitely intrigued.

I had no idea if I'd ever see the tall stranger again, but the ball was already set in motion. My boyfriend and I broke up. Then, fortunately, a few weeks later Jeff walked back into the restaurant. My heart fluttered in my chest. The offer was still good, he said. Had I changed my mind yet?

Our first date was racquetball and lunch. Not exactly high romance. But it didn't matter. I was sold on Jeff's warm, friendly smile and good looks. The guy could talk to anybody about anything. He was also highly ambitious, same as me. He wanted everything excellent that life could offer, and that meant a fantastic job where he made a lot of money so he could afford a nice house, the right cars, and a lot of fun. Jeff was a year older than me and had already graduated from Furman University in Greenville, South Carolina. Now he was flying up the corporate ladder, already promoted to his second position with Riegel Textile. The guy had everything I was looking for. He was husband material, exactly the type of young man you bring home to meet your parents. After our first date I went home, called my mother, and said, "I know who I'm going to marry."

"But what about Bill?" my mother asked.

"I've met someone else," I said. "And I'm positive he's the one."

Jeff and I began spending every minute possible together. I graduated college and started my first job in sales for an office equipment company. A little over a year after our first date, we married and moved to Los Angeles, where Jeff had been transferred.

We threw ourselves into newlywed life. I got a new sales job, and we both dived headlong into our work. Jeff was twenty-five; I was twenty-four. We were making good money for being so young. We bought a condo, ate at all the nicest restaurants, shopped at the finest stores in Beverly Hills and Santa Monica, and went to movies and concerts and to the beach on weekends.

Four years later we had climbed even higher. It was 1986, and we splurged on our first house in an upscale community called Palos Verdes. The house had four bedrooms and an ocean view that took our breath away. We couldn't have been happier.

The only thing that felt weird was having all these empty bedrooms in our new house. It was a problem we planned to remedy soon. We had carefully crafted a mental list of how life was supposed to progress. If we wanted something, we went for it. If we attempted something, we succeeded. We agreed it was time to start a family. I went off birth control. Imagine our surprise six months later when I went in for my normal ob-gyn checkup and found out something was wrong. My doctor was also an infertility specialist. "I think we've got a problem," he said.

The doctor shot dye up into my fallopian tubes. They were as clogged as an LA freeway in rush hour. I felt devastated. Guilty. Flawed. I was never going to be able to give my husband children. Everything in our lives was perfect—except me.

One option was to have surgery to open my tubes. After that we'd have a narrow six-week window to get pregnant before scar tissue closed my tubes again. A pregnancy absolutely needed to take place during that window, because afterward we'd have even less chance of getting pregnant than before. We ruled out that option.

The other option was more experimental. More radical. More controversial.

A test-tube baby. Or, as it came to be known, in vitro fertilization.

Jeff and I both went through a battery of tests. They wanted to make sure Jeff was fertile before putting us through everything else. Jeff was functioning fine, so we began the process. Our marriage turned into a science project. Nine months went by while they prepped my body and we waited. I had hormone shots. Endless bloodwork. Levels were assessed and regulated. We heard a lot of stories about in vitro—some successful, many not. Friends of ours went through the in vitro process, waited a long time without any results, finally adopted a girl, then got pregnant and had quadruplets. Clinic staff knew how difficult the in vitro process can be for a relationship and offered us free marriage counseling, but we shrugged it off. Everything we went after, we accomplished. That was our pattern of approaching life.

Finally my body was ready, the doctors said. Our window of opportunity opened. They filled me with a hormone that causes ovulation. Jeff gave me my last hormone shot at home one night. The next morning we went in, and medical staff retrieved the eggs with an aspirator. They blended the eggs with the sperm, inserted six fertilized eggs inside me, and commanded me to go home and lie in bed for four days with my feet elevated.

I wasn't a Christian back then. Though I was a nominal Catholic, my faith had lapsed by every stretch of the imagination. Mostly, my religious affiliation was only something I wrote on a medical form. Jeff had grown up Baptist, but he had strayed far from his faith during his high school and college years. We were prodigal children running from God, and we were still a long way off.

I distinctly remember, however, while lying in bed during four days of required bed rest, experiencing a moment that could only be described as supernatural. The bedroom window was open, and a breeze was blowing onshore from Catalina Island. As the breeze entered through the window, an incredible peace came over me—a peace like nothing I'd ever felt before. It was like a wild lion exhaling warm breath from heaven. The lion was sitting on a hill somewhere in a country I couldn't imagine, and his breath was carrying an adventure from across the sea. It wasn't a fearful adventure. It was warm, steady, and secure.

I knew I was pregnant.

I absolutely knew it. In that moment, I was as certain of it as I was of my own name. I felt humbled by something I couldn't control, perhaps for the first time ever in my life. Science might have helped produce this pregnancy, but something beyond science had created this life. It was less than four days after the in vitro procedure, but already I knew a child was being wonderfully formed inside me. I knew he or she was already being intricately knit together. I sensed that whoever had sent this breeze through my window could also see this unformed substance, and that he had mapped out every day to come.

Sure, the statistics were against us. We had heard that in vitro fertilization was a long shot, even when everything looked smooth. But we were not people of statistics. We were people of drive and accomplishment. Winners. The possibility of losing the baby never even crossed my mind.

I had no way of knowing some very difficult days would be right around the corner.

CHAPTER 5

Mimicked

Jeff

One and a half weeks after the in vitro fertilization process, we went to South Bay Hospital in Redondo Beach, where doctors did some tests and told us to come back in forty-five minutes. We walked around the block, our cheeks turning bright from the early fall breeze coming off the water, then reentered the building. The nurse met us with a big smile and said, "Good news. You're very pregnant."

"Very pregnant," I said. "What exactly does that mean?"

"Triplets. At least twins."

Cheryl buckled at the knees. We'd known that the process of in vitro fertilization came with a tendency to produce multiple births, but having two or three babies wasn't yet on our radar. We considered ourselves lucky to be pregnant with one child, let alone two. But it made sense. Everything we did, we did in a big way.

As far as a husband is ever conscious of these matters, the pregnancy seemed to go perfectly. All the tests said things were fine. We purposely didn't find out the gender of the children, so we picked names for both boys and girls. Brittany Marie—we were sure of that name. We just liked the sound of Brittany, and Marie was Cheryl's middle name. A boy would be named either Mark Thomas or Adam David. But what if we had two girls? Well, we'd cross that bridge if we came to it.

During her entire pregnancy, Cheryl was confident, but also very cautious. Twins are almost always born at thirty-six weeks or earlier, rather than the normal forty-week gestation period. There's a danger of twins being born underweight, and any number of complications can result if that occurs. Cheryl's high caution put some strain on our marriage, but it wasn't anything I couldn't handle. I reminded myself that a man needs to make certain concessions to his wife when she's pregnant. I was sure everything would return to normal once the babies were born.

Cheryl was a real trouper and carried the babies two weeks longer than scheduled, to thirty-eight weeks, almost full term, which we both were ecstatic about. The doctor scheduled a C-section for July 18, 1988, and we went to the hospital at the appointed hour.

And out they came.

Baby girls!

Two of them!

Each was almost seven pounds. Perfectly healthy. They were gooey and slimy and screaming. Their faces were all scrunched up. The nurse handed them to me, one by one. I thought they were the most beautiful creatures I'd ever seen.

Our first daughter was born at 1 p.m. She was angelic, with dark hair and a perfectly formed head, face, and nose. Brittany Marie.

Our second daughter was born at 1:01 p.m. She was hairless and peachy and looked like a perfect little princess. We'd used up our one girl name, and we had no idea what to call our second child. The nurse wrote "Baby B" on her chart, and that's what we called her for the first couple of days. I was so proud of my two girls. If I had smoked, I would have passed out cigars by the box.

A few days later we settled on the name Lauren Nicole. Lauren sounded sophisticated and fun, like the actress Lauren Bacall. I had known a little girl at the church where I grew up who was named Nicole.

Everybody liked her. The two names sounded good together. Lauren Nicole.

We took our daughters home to our house in Palos Verdes and settled into our new life together. Cheryl took a six-week maternity leave then went back to work. It never crossed my mind that she would do differently. We certainly never talked about it. Hey, with two more mouths to feed, we needed the extra income. We hired a nanny from El Salvador named Zoila who lived with us and took care of the girls during the days. But the girls were not at all fussy. Brittany was more outgoing, with a loud, boisterous cry. She took to me immediately, and we formed a special bond. Brittany was eager to express that she was going places in life—and wanted to get there fast! She fit Team Scruggs to a tee. But Lauren was more timid and shy. She didn't make a lot of noise. I loved her dearly, but it took awhile for her to warm up to me. Lauren was Mommy's girl from moment one.

Cheryl seemed to adjust well to her new role. She often shopped and bought things for the girls. Little dresses and toys. At home she held our daughters, rocked them, and read them books way ahead of their age. She was always hovering around them, giving them the fullest expressions of her love and devotion. Things weren't back to normal in our relationship yet, but I was still confident we were only in the adjustment phase.

XO

One evening at dinner when the girls were about sixteen months old, Zoila kept talking about how she thought Lauren had been looking pale. It took awhile to figure out what she was saying. We thought maybe Lauren was going through a growth spurt. It's hard to tell with babies. But a day later our neighbor said the same thing. She'd seen Lauren out in the yard and thought she looked thin, her skin almost yellow.

We took Lauren to the doctor that afternoon. It was about 3:30 p.m. They tested Lauren's blood and said they'd call us the next day if anything looked out of the ordinary.

At 9 p.m. that same night the phone rang. "I've made an appointment for you first thing tomorrow with a pediatric oncologist," said our doctor. "Now, don't freak out when you go there, but there'll be a lot of kids with cancer at the clinic."

Cancer?!

The mere word sent shivers down our backs.

We took Lauren in for some initial tests. Soon more tests were scheduled. Then even more. For two to three weeks, every two to three days, they called her in for bloodwork. Each time they gave her a little Felix the Cat Band-Aid for her finger. Her health continued to deteriorate, yet everything came back inconclusive. Still, there was one word they kept repeating. At first it was just mentioned in passing, like it was only a remote possibility. Then it was repeated. Until it became a definite possibility.

Leukemia.

They scheduled a spinal tap for our baby.

"You need to hold her down," the doctor said to me. "Hold her down and don't let her move."

Lauren lay facedown on the doctor's table. My hands pressed down tight on her tiny back. She fought, screamed, and tried to twist her face around to see why I was holding her so uncomfortably. The doctor inserted a huge needle into her lower back. Lauren gave one of those cries where a kid screams but doesn't make a noise. Then she let loose. Wailing. Shrieking.

The results from the spinal tap came back: Lauren didn't have leukemia. While we were greatly relieved, we knew she was still in danger.

"We want to give her blood transfusions," the doctor said.

I shook my head no. Lauren's health was still going downhill, but these were the days when we were hearing a lot of news reports about AIDS. Unless blood transfusions were absolutely necessary, we didn't want to risk the procedure. What we wanted were answers. Why was our daughter dying? We waited and paced and wrung our hands helplessly. We checked with neighbors, people we knew, trying to pinpoint and line up donors with Lauren's blood type.

At last a final report came back. A concrete diagnosis was in.

The report said . . . *nothing*.

Lauren was absolutely fine.

Even now, I can't tell you the name of what she'd contracted. It was some rare, super-long, Latin-sounding, one-in-five-billion medical condition. It basically meant that Lauren's hemoglobin levels were stuck—sometimes that happens when you get a virus. All we needed to do was let time pass, and the levels would get unstuck.

Slowly Lauren's color returned to normal. Her weight began increasing as it should. For months afterward we regularly took Lauren to the oncology clinic to get her blood checked. Sometimes two to three times per week. Every test came back perfectly normal. Whatever calamity had visited our family had left as quickly and silently as it had come.

At the clinic, there were always these other little kids. The ones with the sallow faces and bald heads. The scene put a catch in my throat every time. *That could easily have been Lauren*, I thought.

The thought of losing Lauren put a scare into our family that we would not easily shake, but for that next season of life, all seemed right with the world. From then on I held Lauren more closely. I became even more protective of her, perhaps overly protective. My little daughter had experienced a brush with death, and I vowed to do everything in my power to protect her from every evil in the world.

Little did I know, another evil lurked in the shadows. It was just down the line, and I wouldn't see it coming. It would blindside me with such force that our entire world would crumble.

CHAPTER 6

A Jolting Heartache

Jeff

On a Saturday morning in March 1990, Cheryl and I set off for a bike ride on the beach—something we'd done countless times before. Cheryl and I strapped the twins into their car seats, loaded our bicycles onto the rack on our car, and drove from our home in Palos Verdes down to Redondo Beach, just a couple of miles away. We unhooked the bicycles, put helmets on the girls, and each strapped a daughter to the toddler seat fastened to the back of our bikes. Cheryl took Brittany. I took Lauren. As I doubled-checked Lauren's straps to make sure she was secure, I tickled her underneath her chin. "Again, Dada," she said, grinning and giggling.

The girls were dressed like warm little berries in matching OshKosh B'gosh outfits with different colors—Brittany in purple, Lauren in pink. The girls wore a lot of OshKosh outfits. Easygoing overalls. Fleecy jackets. Colorful knit tops. I'd been working as a sales executive with the company for the past few years, and I thrived in the job. It felt like the company was doing something good—we were helping families have fun. But mostly, it was a career that seemed to be leading somewhere. The harder I worked, the more money I made. And that suited my life's goals exactly.

With the sun full on my face that day, I chuckled to think of how perfectly my life was turning out. I had everything any man could ever want, or so I thought. I had two miraculous daughters, one of whom had beaten the odds against a leukemia scare. I had a gorgeous wife, and she and I got along fantastically. Cheryl worked hard as a sales rep for Konica Business Machines, and with our two combined incomes, we were able to do anything we wanted. We had the right cars. We had the right house. We were going places in a really big way.

Cheryl, the girls, and I set out on our family bike ride. I rode first, and Cheryl brought up the rear. The twins laughed and cooed from their seats. They could already talk to each other in long, babbling toddler conversations. They really seemed to be communicating, even finishing each other's sentences like mind readers. Cheryl and I pedaled along the serpentine bike path that parallels the beach up through Hermosa.

"I'm getting a little tired," Cheryl shouted to me. "You think we could stop for a while and just talk?"

"We're almost to Manhattan Beach," I called over my shoulder. "We can make the state park if we hurry."

No way was I stopping. The morning was perfect. It wasn't too windy. The sun was warming the waves, drying up the mist along the shores. The girls were happy. The whole purpose of coming to the beach was to ride our bikes, wasn't it? To go places and do things. Cheryl didn't say anything else, and I didn't give it a second thought.

We made the state park in good time, circled back south, and pedaled into the city. After riding a few blocks, we stopped at our favorite breakfast joint. I had worked up an appetite and ordered a full farmer's breakfast with two slices of ham, three links of sausage, three eggs, hash browns, and toast. The girls munched on waffles and drank milk from their bottles. Cheryl ate half a bagel and a slice of fruit.

"Jeff," she said, then paused.

"Yeah?" I looked up between bites of eggs.

"Um." Cheryl straightened her napkin. "It's . . . uh, never mind."

"What?"

"Nothing." She gave a half smile. "It's a perfect morning, isn't it? That's all I was going to say." She turned her attention back to the girls, picked up Brittany's bottle, which had fallen, and wiped Lauren's syrupy face.

Weird, I thought. *Maybe Cheryl's tired. Or maybe it's just one of her moods.* I loved my wife. I truly did. But I didn't always understand her. Sometimes when I came home, I'd find her wiping her eyes quickly or blowing her nose like she'd just been crying or something. She never talked about what was bothering her. If I pressed her for answers, she always said things were fine.

We finished our family bike ride and went home. The next day I was set to go golfing with a couple of buddies while Cheryl stayed home with the girls. On Sunday afternoon I gathered my golf stuff and went upstairs to tell Cheryl I was leaving. Our bedroom door was closed, and I paused outside before going in. Cheryl was on the phone with someone. She must have thought I'd already left. I could hear her speaking in low tones. Muffled. Guarded. I opened the door.

"It's my mother," she said, then hung up.

Cheryl had been crying.

"Honey, what's wrong?" I said, glancing at my watch. I didn't want to miss my tee time.

"Jeff . . ." After a brief pause, the words tumbled out. "I'm just not sure I can do it anymore," she said.

"What are you talking about?" I tried to read her expression, but Cheryl wasn't looking at me.

Then came the words that would change our lives.

"I don't think I love you, Jeff. In fact, I don't think I've ever loved you." The bluntness of my wife's words hit the air in our bedroom with a thud.

I was stunned. Our marriage was solid. Even my buddies said how they envied what Cheryl and I had together. She must have just been tired. "Cheryl, what are you saying? How long have you felt like this?" I pressed for more answers, but it was like a television set had suddenly turned off. I could see Cheryl right in front of me. But she had rolled over and turned her face to the wall. Conversation over.

There didn't seem to be anything else to do, so I went out with my friends. I didn't shrug off what Cheryl had said. But I was shocked and couldn't believe we'd just had that conversation. Either I'd been the world's most clueless man, or Cheryl had been frighteningly good at hiding the truth about herself. Over the next few days Cheryl and I tried to talk a few times, but we couldn't seem to discuss anything of substance. I convinced her we should try counseling. It seemed like the right way to tackle a challenge head-on. I made some calls, and we went once or twice. But the whole process of opening up to a stranger felt stiff and reserved. Cheryl's answers were all one-worded, vague, almost like she was purposely avoiding any depth. Quickly I became convinced that the counseling was a waste of money. We stopped going.

One Monday a couple of weeks later, my manager called me into his office. The conversation at work was equally blunt. "Need you out in Dallas," my manager said. "As quick as you can move." I thought Cheryl would be upset to leave the life we'd made for ourselves in Los Angeles, but when I told her about the transfer, she seemed ecstatic. Almost relieved.

"A change sounds perfect," she said and gave me a quick little hug. Her enthusiasm for my career made me happy. I almost felt a cautious hope. We still hadn't talked much about our marriage, but I thought maybe the move would be good for us.

Notice of the transfer came in April 1990, and we sold our house soon after. The girls turned two in July, and we moved to Dallas at the beginning of August. We settled into a condo temporarily while we consulted an architect who drew up plans to build our dream home. We'd build it right on the Queens Course of the Gleneagles Country Club.

For Cheryl, who loved to golf, it was going to be awesome. Her dad owned a nine-hole golf course in the small town of Lodi, Ohio, where Cheryl had grown up. Her family lived next to the course, and Cheryl had golfed her whole childhood and throughout college. Now she could walk outside and go golfing anytime she wanted.

For a few weeks all seemed well. But Cheryl still cried a lot. I assumed it was the stress of moving and taking care of the twins. Dallas, I was sure, would give us the fresh start we needed.

Our friends invited us to their church. It was Presbyterian, nothing I was used to, and I think we went at first just to be polite. But the decision made sense. If there were still problems in our marriage, church would surely help. I wasn't against church or spirituality or even Jesus. He just didn't fit into my life's plans. I wouldn't exactly call the church we tried out "captivating." It was liturgical in style, more formal than anything I'd ever experienced in the churches of West Virginia I'd attended as a child. But Cheryl seemed to like the services okay, and anything she wanted, I would do for her.

We didn't have our nanny anymore, and Cheryl quit work so she could stay home with the girls. Fortunately my job was going gangbusters. They loved me at OshKosh. Nothing would stop me from reaching the sky.

Five months after we moved to Dallas, our McMansion was finished. We ditched the condo, hauled all our stuff out of storage, and moved into our new home. The place was absolutely perfect. We had all the room in the world to fill with stuff. On Valentine's Day 1991, right after we moved in, I surprised Cheryl with a brand-new set of Ping Eye2s, the best set of golf clubs money could buy at the time. I hid them in our bed, right between the sheets. That evening Cheryl climbed under the covers, gave a little gasp, and let out a huge smile. "These are wonderful, Jeff," she said. "Really wonderful." She didn't say anything else. She didn't even kiss me. But I patted myself on the back anyway. I was surely the best husband ever.

A month later I was upstairs reading the girls a bedtime story when the doorbell rang. Cheryl was downstairs, so I assumed she'd get it. The doorbell rang again. I turned the page, stopped right in the middle of the kitty and the horsey on their way to the circus, and muttered my frustration. The doorbell rang a third time.

"Why isn't she getting it?" I asked under my breath, and then, "Hang on, girls. Daddy will be right back."

"I wanna go," Lauren said. She clutched my arm with a birdlike grip. The doorbell rang a fourth time.

"Sure, sure," I said. "C'mon." I picked up Lauren, tucked her under my arm, and climbed down the stairs. I could just make out a uniformed hat through the glass at the top of the door.

"Jeff Scruggs?" the man said when I opened the door.

"That's me." I looked at the man and raised an eyebrow. "What's wrong, officer?" It was the county sheriff.

"These are for you." The sheriff handed me a file. "Sign here, here, and here." He pointed. I paused for a moment, then obediently signed. The sheriff turned without a word and walked back to his squad car.

I could still think clearly enough to close the front door.

I could think to pull Lauren closer to me and walk up the stairs, still holding her in my arms.

I could think to tuck her and her sister into bed.

I even finished the girls' bedtime story. The kitty and the horsey found their way to the circus and had a terrific time. I sang the girls their songs. I made sure their night-light was switched on. I kissed their toothpaste-flavored lips goodnight.

Then I closed the door, my heart pounding, and flew down the stairs. Our bedroom door was closed tight. I barged in.

"Cheryl! You've got to be kidding."

My wife lay on the bed, her eyes half closed. She looked at me coldly. Silently. Then shook her head. She said nothing.

There was absolutely no discussion ahead of time.

No months of arguments leading up to one final confrontation.

No shouting. No fights.

No clue.

That's how my wife served me with divorce papers.

XO

We sold our dream home on the golf course in June 1992. Cheryl bought a much smaller house, and I rented one five minutes away from her so I could stay as close to the girls as possible. We never said the actual word *divorce* to the girls. At their age, I doubt if they would have understood what it meant. But we brought them together and sat them down and said, "Mommy and Daddy aren't going to live together anymore."

Those were the words we used. Brittany ran to her room and slammed the door. Lauren went and sat in a corner in the guest bathroom and wouldn't come out. They understood exactly what was happening.

"They're going to be fine," Cheryl said.

"Right." I was so angry I could spit. "Just fine."

Neither of us moved out until we had to. We slept in separate bedrooms; that was a given. When the day came, the movers arrived with two big trucks and began to separate the belongings of each room in our perfect McMansion, according to our instructions. Couches. Dressers. Desks. Tables. Clothes. Lamps. TVs. Golf clubs. Our whole life, ripped in two. Even the movers couldn't handle it. "This is the saddest thing I've ever seen," one said to me. He was sweaty and bald with a huge stomach. "Dude, you two are the perfect couple. Have you ever thought about buying her flowers?"

"Thanks," I said. "But it's way past flowers now."

On August 21, 1992, our divorce was finalized, just a month after the twins turned four. We had been married for ten years, but it was now officially over. There was no more Mr. and Mrs. Jeff and Cheryl Scruggs.

We put a visitation schedule in place. It was standard custody procedure. I had the girls the first, third, and fifth weekends of the month, as well as the Wednesdays and Thursdays during the weeks when I had them for the weekend, or Mondays and Tuesdays if they were at their mother's for the weekend. It sounded complicated at first, but it soon became routine.

Cheryl was amicable. Polite. Gracious. A perfect ex-wife. There were never any arguments between us. Even with our family in shambles, we still did everything perfectly. We even had the world's perfect divorce.

A month went by, and then another. Six months passed. Eight months. A year. This was real. Very real. A broken family was our new permanent reality. Even the world's perfect divorce was still horrible.

A friend and I split the cost on a small lake house a couple of hours away from Dallas. I figured I could use it for vacations in the years to come. The girls and I had a ball together there—waterskiing, swimming, paddling a canoe. I bought the lake house out of love for my daughters, but I also bought it out of anger toward my ex-wife. There was no way she'd ever go there. Not in a million years. It became representative to me of the one place in my life she could never ruin.

Strangely enough, both Cheryl and I kept going to church. She told me she'd started attending a women's Bible study. Although she had a marginal religious background, she'd never actually studied the Word of God before. Until now, she'd never been taught how a person could have a personal relationship with God through Jesus Christ. For the first time some things were beginning to click for her, she added. I just nodded. *Too little, too late*, I thought.

I began making some spiritual strides of my own. The youth pastor asked me to help out as a sponsor with the church's high school group, and I agreed. Initially I just did crowd control. I'd show up at the church on Wednesday evenings and hang out, herding the kids from their game times to their discussion times, whatever needed to be done. About a year later, the youth pastor asked me to lead a boys' book study, so I bought a ten-pack of *Disciplines of a Godly Man* by Kent Hughes and gave a copy to each of the guys. Every Sunday night I'd read a chapter in preparation and then lead the boys through the chapter the following Wednesday night. "Train yourself to be godly," I read. "For physical training is of some value, but godliness has value for all things, holding promise for both the present life and the life to come" (1 Timothy 4:7-8, NIV). It was an eye-opening book for me. "Guys," I told them one night, "I might be thirty-six years old, but when it comes to learning this stuff, I'm only three days ahead of you."

On a Saturday morning, a little more than a year after the divorce, I took the girls to a city park. I brought a little brown paper sack with some cheese sticks, crackers, and juice boxes inside. After the girls and I ate our snacks, we hiked down around the creek that ran through the park. We spotted crawdads and found a frog, its eyes bulging, but didn't try to capture it. We looked for imaginary dinosaur prints in the brown, suburban sand and picked up little rocks and pretended they were long lost arrowheads.

After half an hour we hiked back to the main area of the park, and

I sat on a bench as the girls ran to the playground equipment. Brittany swung arm over arm across the monkey bars, while Lauren climbed to the highest rung of the biggest slide.

"Lauren!" I called. "Be careful! You, too, Brittany—always be careful!"

But the damage had already been done.

That day, they wouldn't fall from the monkey bars or tumble off the slide.

They would simply look at me, their father, their eyes full of joy, yet also full of unmistakable sadness.

CHAPTER 7

Bittersweet Years

Brittany (Lauren's twin)

To say I feel a sense of responsibility for my twin sister, Lauren, is an understatement. When we were four years old and our parents divorced, I took on the role of the eldest child, the rescuer, even though I'm older than Lauren by only one minute. After our parents no longer lived together, so many juggling pins of uncertainty were tossed into the air. We couldn't catch enough of them to make sense of our lives. But we needed to keep going forward, despite our wounded hearts.

As sisters, we were inseparable, more so after the divorce than ever. A huge part of our security as kids was knowing we always had a familiar friend nearby. Even from the moment Lauren and I were born, we shared an ultra-close connectedness. No matter what season of life we were in, Lauren and I never fought. We were never jealous of each other. We never experienced any of the normal sibling rivalry so many sisters struggle with. Lauren and I could lock eyes and remind ourselves of an experience without even talking. We could tell a joke without words and then push it further until we were both in hysterics, still never uttering a single word. We could envision the same mental image without speaking it—it was completely unfair to play Catch Phrase against us. That's how the growing up years went for Lauren and me. We were always on the same side. I didn't know how to be myself if Lauren wasn't there. Sometimes it felt as if we were the same person.

During the night of the propeller accident, as we all prayed so hard for Lauren's recovery, both good news and bad news circled back to us with each team of surgeons that worked on her. We knew Lauren's condition had stabilized and that she had escaped death, but the full extent of her injuries was being discovered little by little. The hardest news came after Lauren's brain surgery. When the propeller had smashed down on her head, more than one blade had hit her. It had taken only a miniscule fraction of a second for her body to jolt away on reflex, but the damage had already been done. Part of her skull was shattered; the fragmented bones were pressing into her brain. "Brain injuries are always tricky," the neurosurgeon said to us in the waiting room. His face was grave. We could tell he was trying to brace us for the worst. "Lauren might never form a complete sentence again. Even if she recovers well, she might have a vastly different personality."

I couldn't go there. I just couldn't. I desperately needed my sister to be the same beautiful, vibrant person she had always been—in mind as well as body. I needed to know that she was still LoLo.

LoLo—that's what our family always called her when we were young. Or just *Lo* for short. Mom started it when we were little, maybe three. The nickname stuck. It was just part of our fun. After the divorce, Dad would pick up uncooked ravioli from a specialty store next to his office in Dallas. He'd bring it home, and he, Lo, and I would hang out in his kitchen, pretending to be gourmet chefs in the fanciest restaurant in all of Italy. He'd screw up his face into this hoity-toity grimace and speak fluent fake Italian. "Hey-ah you-ah, you are both so vehry goo-oo-ood loo-oo-ook-ing. From now on I will call you Lorenessimo." He pointed a spatula at Lauren. "And I will call you Brittchessi." He looked at me.

"All right, Dad," I said and giggled. "As long as we can call you Dachessi."

That's how we related in our family, even though we weren't all together anymore. It wasn't like we were sad every moment of every day. We always had a lot of fun together: us with Mom, us with Dad. We knew our parents still loved us deeply, and they worked hard to provide us with the most normal childhood possible.

After we grew up, Lauren and I eventually went our separate ways—but only to a point. When Lauren interned in the fashion industry, I interned at an inner-city ministry. When I was twenty-two, I married my college sweetheart, Shaun Morgan, the most wonderful man in the world. I'd forgotten it by then, but the strange homeless man's prediction from years before had come true for me. He said I'd live a life of kindness with the support of a man who'd help bring me to the top of that goal. Shaun was that man; I knew without a doubt. But even with that amount of confidence securing the decision in my mind, a month before Shaun and I got married, I had a little meltdown. I just couldn't bear the thought of leaving Lauren all alone, of living life without her so close by. I kept thinking, *Oh my gosh, is Lauren going to be okay?* When I confessed my fears to my sister, the two of us had a long and beneficial conversation. At the end she gave a low, bemused laugh, and said, "Brittany, I'm going to be just fine. I'm really excited for you guys!"

The funny thing about my husband, Shaun, is that, personality-wise, he *is* Lauren, almost exactly. I married a male version of my sister. And Shaun has no problem being married to a twin. For instance, for birthdays he'll do something special for both Lo and me. He realizes we've grown up always thinking of the date as "our" birthday, never individually.

Lauren welcomed Shaun into our family just as warmly. Their mutual respect was particularly evident after the accident. As Lauren began to recover, Shaun was one of the people she listened to most closely. Early on in the hospital stay, she slurred her words while regaining her speech. Sometimes she added extra syllables to words, almost like English was a foreign language and she didn't have the idioms quite right yet. She nicknamed Shaun "Bosser Cracker," a combination of "boss" and "crack the whip," we think. Each morning Shaun went to the hospital for an hour while Mom or Dad went back to their hotel or I went back to my house to take a shower and get some sleep. His shift came before he went to work, right after Lauren woke up. She was often most alert then. "Hey Bosser Cracker," she'd slur, and Shaun would smile, gently rub her forehead on the undamaged side, and work with her to perform some simple movements before she would fall in and out of sleep.

As the days unfolded, I began to adore Shaun's close concern for Lauren. It showed how he was assuming the same responsibilities I'd always assumed. He was becoming the older sibling just like me, looking out for Lauren just like I've always tried to do, even in the times I couldn't be there for her.

Not that Lauren always needed watching. As an adult she's responsible and entrepreneurial, and growing up she was a highly capable child. Intelligent. Funny. Creative. It's just that the pattern of me watching out for her was established early. Sure, the divorce factored into the equation, but even when Lo and I were babies, I took the lead. I hovered over Lauren like a little mother. She walked before I did. Even ran at nine months. But she didn't start talking until she was good and ready, around two years of age. I didn't walk until our first birthday, but I would babble up a storm long before I could walk. Lauren was always the cautious one, the shy one. I was confident and outgoing, eager to lead the way. If people asked us our names, I'd make the introductions. "I'm Brittany," I'd say, and then add, "and her name is LoLo."

People said we were as cute as little princesses, and I guess we were. Mom cut our hair back then, and Lauren and I wore it the same way— thick bangs, hair to our shoulders. Lauren was a tiny beanpole. Almost frail looking. For the longest time, she couldn't gain weight. I was fuller. Stronger.

The fall after we turned five, we both started kindergarten at Daffron Elementary, a few blocks away from our mom's house in Plano. For the first day of school, Mom had bought us dresses that matched in every way except the colors.

For some reason when it came to kindergarten, school administrators thought it would be best if they split us up. Lauren went one way. I went another. I hated the thought of Lauren being alone. Who was going to watch out for her if I wasn't there? On the first morning

Mrs. Scarborough sat our class down on the rug in a semicircle in front of our desks to take roll call. She looked up midstream from her counting and said in a kind but firm voice, "Children, it looks like we have one extra student in class."

I raised my hand. "My sister is with me," I said confidently. "We don't ever want to be apart." Lauren had snuck out of her classroom and was hiding behind my back.

Mostly those were good years. Every summer we went to Dad's lake house. We'd learned how to water-ski when we were four. Dad held us in the water while his friend drove the ski boat. Going to the lake house was always a fun adventure. We had bunk beds in our rooms where we created forts and caves with blankets and pillows and made up stories of princesses, knights, and dragons. We made drip castles on the beach and dug up orange-brown clay when the water was low, shaping the clay into bowls and drying them in the sun. Emma and Carson, the children of Dad's friend, often stayed at the lake house with us. Emma was just a little older than us; Carson, a little younger. One of our favorite games was hiding from Carson, a sweet kid, but always full of brotherly annoyance. With Dad's help, we hammered together a tree house high in the hollow of the oldest tree in the neighborhood, a beautiful two-hundred-year-old oak, and passed down a bucket on a rope to bring up our treasures. One year during a tornado, that old oak toppled over, which made us all cry. We couldn't fathom why such strength would fail us, why something that beautiful would ever need to die.

Mom took us to Sunday school regularly. A change was stirring within her, although we might not have been able to articulate it that way. She read her Bible all the time. She journaled and prayed and went to Bible studies at the church. In second grade I followed her new example of spiritual growth and decided to trust Jesus as my Lord and Savior. Trees topple over, I reasoned, and even parents let you down, but surely God is trustworthy. Lauren was thinking the same spiritual thoughts. She told me about them, but I'm not sure she would have initiated becoming a Christian unless I did it first. We both made the decision—individually, and yet together. It was real, a lifelong journey we'd begun, even though we were only seven.

After that, Mom bought us each a Bible and a journal and taught us how to write out our prayers so our minds wouldn't wander. In her house was a big, comfy tan couch. In the evenings, we would curl up together against the floral pattern and read, watch TV, or think big thoughts.

"Mom," I said one night out of the blue. "Do you think you and Dad will ever get back together?"

She smiled. "It would take a miracle." That was all she said.

Later that night, tucked under the covers, Lauren and I held a private sisters' meeting. If it was going to take a miracle, then we'd pray for one. We vowed to pray every night for Mom and Dad to get married again. We'd pray for the rest of our lives if needed. But as soon as we made our vow, we had to laugh at the thought. Who were we kidding? We knew how far-fetched a prayer it was. It was going to take a God-size miracle to ever bring about something so ridiculous.

In the meantime, we planned to cooperate with God any way he might want to work. Lo and I watched the movie *The Parent Trap*—not the modern remake, but the 1961 version where Hayley Mills plays identical twins (she plays both roles) who scheme to get their parents back together. Our mouths hung open at the brilliance of the idea. We put our heads together and figured out how we could do the same thing. We kept our big secret for days while we worked out all the kinks. That next Friday when Mom dropped us off at Dad's house, we instructed our parents to hug us both at the same time and give us big kisses. As our parents moved in for the clinch, Lauren and I counted to three and ducked down, hoping they'd accidentally kiss each other.

Drat! They were too smart for us.

Lo and I realized other complications existed with our plan. Much bigger complications. Mom had a boyfriend, Todd, and he wasn't going away. He didn't live in the same city as we did, and we didn't know much about him, but he came over to our house a few times. Mom never talked about him to us, but we knew he was in the picture somehow.

Dad dated a few girlfriends too. One was blonde and fine-featured and looked eerily similar to our mom. I can't remember her name, but she even came to the lake house with us once. "Why is she here?" Lauren hissed when the woman was out of hearing range. But there was no answer. This was the new normal, and we had to get used to it. And so the bittersweet years went by.

Sure, we had fun. We played in the backyard and rode bikes and busied ourselves learning new activities like softball, soccer, gymnastics, and art. We both took piano lessons for years. Each year at recital time we played a duet together, but piano was never a deep love for Lauren, not like it was for me. When life got hard, I pounded on the ivories, pouring out my emotions on this wonderful melodic medium that reacted, note by note.

While I channeled my feelings into music, Lo preferred painting classes. Her art teacher was this wide-smiled hippie named Dawn. She was very artsy, the kind of woman with clay under her fingernails from throwing pots on her own wheel. "Just be as free as you can," she told Lauren, and the art teacher's words surrounded Lo and worked their magic. Dawn released Lauren from shyness like no other person could. Hours went by in the classroom, and Lauren immersed herself in paintings, sketches, acrylics, pottery. I think it became rehabilitation for my sister. Whenever we came to the classroom to get her, she never wanted to leave. Each week she counted down the days until she could go again. Lauren's favorite animal was a pig, which she felt funny about. Other little girls were enamored with horses, bunnies, or puppies. But Lauren saw something poignant about a pig. She liked the quirky *pinkness* of a pig. Dawn encouraged Lauren to paint all the pigs she could ever imagine. Wild pigs. Flying pigs. Pigs that danced and sparkled and laughed. And Lo did.

XO

Our nightly prayers seemed to hit a brick wall. No matter how hard we tried, we couldn't accept the fact that our parents were completely, legally, irrevocably no longer together. No matter how much time passed, it never sat right in our hearts. Year after year after year, the wound was a raw scrape that refused to scab over. If we were at Dad's house for the night, we missed Mom. If we were at Mom's house, we missed Dad. Our parents tried as hard as they could. We sincerely thanked them for that. When it came to parenting, they maintained the best working relationship possible. For our sakes, they purposely lived only five minutes apart. They were always on the phone with each other, talking about someone's missing library book or who needed the other half of an outfit. If Lauren or I were having a hard night and missed the other parent, Dad would call Mom and she'd come over and tuck us in, or the other way around.

But it never got easier.

We weren't angry at our parents. That wasn't the feeling. It was more a continual longing—that's what echoed through our souls. As kids growing up in a divorced family, we were always living out of a suitcase. We didn't have a home. We had *two* homes. You'd think that would make us feel lucky, but it didn't. You don't want two homes as a kid. You just want one.

Holidays and vacations were often the hardest—like the Fourth of July when we were eight. Dad had custody of us for the long weekend. The plan was to head to the lake house to watch fireworks. But Lauren didn't want to go. I mean, she did. But she didn't. She pulled me aside and whispered, "Brittany, Mom's going to be all alone this weekend."

"I know. But it's Dad's weekend with us. Don't worry. We'll have fun there."

"I can't bear the thought of Mom being all by herself."

I sighed. "I know. Me too."

Late that Friday afternoon, before we left for the weekend, something burrowed its way into my little twin sister's mind. She stepped out and made her own decision, maybe for the first time ever. She made a bold choice without me speaking on her behalf, and I knew there was no use trying to change her mind.

"I'm going with Mom." Lauren's chin was firm with resolution. "You stay with Dad. He'll understand."

Mom didn't try to sway Lauren's decision. Neither did Dad. There was never any open conflict in their relationship, not as far as we observed. Lauren went with Mom, and they watched a community fireworks display somewhere in downtown Dallas. I went with Dad, and we sat on the dock together at the lake house, watching the sky burst into colors all around the dark water.

That holiday weekend was neither sad nor happy. It simply reflected the reality of our lives: we were a family divided. That night I awoke in the blackness in a sweat and fought my way out from under the covers. I switched on the bedside lamp and noticed how bare and alone it was above me in the bunk where Lauren usually slept. I bunched my pillow and doubled my prayers, the same prayers Lauren and I prayed every night. But I was hit anew with the fact we all needed to accept: my parents' divorce was real, and it bore all the marks of forever. With the night at its darkest moment, I doubted if the dawn would ever arrive.

CHAPTER 8

Here Comes the Sun

Lauren

After the accident I lay in critical condition in the hospital for days, so I was told later. Mostly I was unconscious. Not in a coma. Just out of it. Heavily sedated. My body in shock.

I don't remember anything from that time in my life. No lights. No sounds. No visits to heaven or conversations with God. I didn't know what an hour was, or a day, or how many of either had passed, or what it meant for time to continue forward. There was nothing in my mind's eye. Not even darkness. My thoughts, my memories, my hopes, my ambitions were simply, completely, erased.

As I fought to come to, it slowly felt like the electricity was being turned on in my brain. It wasn't an immediate current. More like a string of old Christmas tree lights that sparked and fizzled. That eccentric haze was the most frightening part of it, if I could even consciously remember what fear was. I fought to remember what it means to be alive. To have an awareness of myself. As the sparks and fizzles grew stronger, I began to know who I was and know that I was living, but I couldn't articulate in my mind what made me different from an inanimate object like a bedpost or a bowl of cereal.

I began to see shadows. Shapes. Jittery at first, moving—then slow, blurry. Then dreams, I think. Then shadows again. The fog in my mind felt so thick. The blankness so . . . blank. While in this swirling semiconscious state, I feared that I would never again get back to where I needed to be. That I would never again be *me*. One of my earliest moments of consciousness in the hospital—if I could even call it consciousness yet—was an urge to tell somebody something. I needed to speak important words to somebody I knew. But I couldn't imagine what a person was, or what a word was, or what communication was, if that makes any sense. All I could think to do—if I was thinking at all—was to keep fighting forward.

I remember experiencing a similarly difficult-to-describe fear when I was a child. Not a war-zone type of fear where my parents screamed at each other. In this case it was more a silent-but-sinister type of fear. Some nights when the lights were off—I don't exactly know how to articulate it—something lurked in my mom's house. A genuine presence of evil. Once, around midnight, I sensed the presence as I lay in my pajamas. The fear paralyzed me. I prayed to God, then screamed out loud, which brought Mom running. "There's someone in here!" I shouted. "You gotta check under the bed! All the closets! Everywhere!" Mom combed through the whole house and found nothing. The presence was gone then. But what I'd felt was something different than just a normal childhood fear of the boogeyman. A residual evil surrounded the house. Something was fighting to steal from us, kill us, or destroy us. I don't know any other way to describe it than that.

Both my parents worked hard at providing a secure environment for Brittany and me—as best they could, anyway, while living apart. When we were little, we kids slept in Mom's bed most nights when we were over at her house. When we were at Dad's, we cajoled him into moving Brittany's bed into my bedroom. We explained to Dad how we wanted to turn the other bedroom into our playroom, and that was true, to an extent. But mostly it was because Brittany and I didn't want to go to sleep with no one else around.

To this day, if I hear the sound of a blow-dryer, it puts me to sleep in two minutes. Mornings when we were at Mom's house, I'd wake up early while Mom would be getting dressed. I'd amble over to her bathroom and flop down on the carpeted floor next to where she stood in front of the sink. "Just relax for a few more minutes, Lo," she'd say and nuzzle my back with her toes. I'd fall fast asleep again, right where I lay. Sometimes she'd turn her dryer on medium-warm and blow the balmy air all over me in my nightgown. It was the most relaxing, comforting feeling in the world.

Dad was the master craftsman at putting us to bed. One evening when we were teeny-tiny, we asked him to sing us a good-night song. He mumbled a few lines of a 1970s rock ballad, something from his college days. Then he must have realized where he was, because he changed directions and broke into the only children's song that came to his mind: "Edelweiss" from *The Sound of Music*. Dad must not have remembered all the words, so he made some up as he went along. The last line stuck with us though, because he had so obviously changed it. *Bless Brittany and Lauren forever.* The song, sung in Dad's special way, became a nightly routine—until we hit junior high. At that point, we decided we were too old for Dad to be singing to us before bed anymore.

Mom and Dad established routines that made Britt and me feel secure in their love for us; yet I still craved the normalcy I saw between my friends and their married parents. While both my parents might come to a school open house, I knew one of them would be going home alone afterward. If a friend invited me to a sleepover later in the month, I had to do some calculations to figure out which parent I'd be staying with then—so I'd know who to ask for permission.

Britt and I never gave up hope, though. We kept praying every night. Praying, praying, praying. Always praying for the same thing. Every once in a while we saw glimmers of hope. Sometimes Mom and Dad shared a meal together at the same house. It's hard to budget and cook for just one person, they said. If one was dropping us off at the other parent's house, it just made good economic sense to all eat from the same pot. At other times, whichever parent stayed for dinner would linger for an hour or two afterward, and that made sense too. Brittany and I silently compared notes and both vowed, without speaking, to always ask the other parent to put us to bed if we could get away with it. Other times our maneuverings were bolder. We'd call up a parent and directly invite him or her over to dinner at the other parent's house. "C'mon Dad," we'd sing out gleefully. "We're eating your favorite tonight—it's *ravioli*!" Sometimes we went to baseball games or to the movies as a family—it made sense to all buy tickets together. We celebrated Christmas once with all of us over at Dad's place. That way Mom and Dad didn't need to cart all the presents to two houses, they explained. One time Dad took us on a trip to Colorado, and Mom came along. We were puzzled at first because no explanation was given. Then we were excited, but soon everything turned weird. Dad was in a bad mood most of the trip. I'm not sure if he actually wanted Mom there or not.

We sure wished they could bury the hatchet. Or whatever they needed to do to work out their problems. Living out of a suitcase became more frustrating for me, not less, as the years went on. One evening when we were eleven, Brittany and I were staying at Dad's house. Our good friend Erika was there, and we girls were all playing dress-up. (Actually, we called it "makeover.") I really wanted a certain shirt to match the pair of pants I was wearing. But my shirt was at Mom's house, and my pants were at Dad's house. In my eleven-year-old reasoning, nothing else in the closets would do. Not even Brittany could coax me back from the ledge. In my mind, the whole mess was an indication of how wearisome our living situation was. The things we held most important were never where we needed them to be. I started crying and wouldn't stop. Dad came in to see what was wrong. "Honey, I'm sure you can wear another shirt," he said.

Now, we've all known Erika for years. She has auburn hair (some would call it red), and she's feisty and not afraid to speak her mind. She is also close enough to me and Britt—both in age and depth of friendship—to be considered almost part of our family. While Dad was trying to comfort me, Erika suddenly let loose on him. It clearly had nothing to do with clothes. "Jeff, this is ridiculous! I don't understand why you and Cheryl aren't back together. You know you love her, and she loves you. You guys are happier than most married couples I know!"

Dad stood a moment, his jaw hanging slack. Then he backed up without saying a word, went into his bedroom, and closed the door. I swear I heard him crying.

Oh man, I absolutely loved Erika right then. She'd said exactly what we'd dreamed of saying for years.

XO

That summer Brittany and I attended Sky Ranch Camp, about two hours away. We were both, most certainly, going through our awkward phase. My hair was cut to my chin, and I still had chunky bangs. I was taller but still superskinny, not an ounce of curve anywhere. Brittany had more of what she called "baby fat" and always wore her hair up in a ponytail. Neither of us had any concept of trying to look cute. Sure, we were aware of boys, but they were just the species who hogged the tetherball after lunch. Our main interests lay squarely in candy, hanging out with our girlfriends, and having a good time.

Brittany and I spent the week doing what we always did at Sky Ranch. We went horseback riding and hiking and smelled the pine trees around the campfire and ate s'mores. At the end of camp, we stood in the pickup area, kicked rocks with our shoes, and wondered which parent was going to pick us up. We were both thoroughly worn out from all the fun and, as is the case with camp, thoroughly filthy.

"I thought Mom was supposed to pick us up," I said.

"No, it's Dad. I'm sure of it," Brittany said.

Dad's car pulled off the road and into the lot. "Hey, they're both here," I said. Brittany and I exchanged glances. We hugged them both, chucked our duffel bags into the trunk, and bounded into the backseat.

"Sheesh," Mom said. "No offense, but you guys could both use showers. Lo—is that a piece of Jolly Rancher stuck in your hair?"

I just grinned. We drove another mile down the road, and Brittany and I jabbered about our counselor and how she could flip her eyelids inside out. We'd just begun to holler one of the songs we'd learned during the week when Dad jumped in and cut our singing short. He had a strange gleam in his eye. "Mom and I have a surprise for you," he said into the rearview mirror. "But we can't tell you what it is until we get home."

"What is it?" Brittany asked quickly.

"Yeah, tell us!" I chimed in.

"Nope, not just yet," Mom said. Her eyes bore the same strange twinkle as Dad's.

We shrugged and started singing again, belting out a loud chorus of "King Jesus is all, my all in all." I wondered if maybe the surprise was that we were going on another vacation somewhere right after camp. Maybe Mom would come with us again. Maybe it was Colorado. *Oooh, Colorado in summertime would be cool*, I thought.

As soon as we pulled into the driveway at Dad's house, we jumped out and lugged our bags to the laundry room while Dad put the keys away. Mom poured us all glasses of orange juice. Brittany slammed the washer's lid. "Okay, time's up," she said. "What's your big surprise?"

The room grew quiet. Dad set down his glass of juice. "Well, while you guys were gone, your mom and I talked about a lot of things."

I held my breath. My heart began to pound.

Dad swallowed. "It's this. Your mom and I really love each other." Another huge pause. "And . . . well . . . we've decided to get remarried."

For one perfect second, time stopped. The world actually quit spinning. The sun stood still.

Brittany let out a little gasp, then totally lost it, crying, screaming, melting into a puddle in Mom and Dad's arms.

I was like, "What? No way!" then went completely hyper. I sprinted around the house, leaping over chairs, flying around our coffee table, jumping, dancing, skipping, shouting. *Wha-hoooo-ooooo!*

Mom and Dad had been divorced for seven years. God had brought about a change in their lives and prompted what we'd all once thought was impossible. Our parents' reconciliation was real.

Three months later, the four of us gathered at a tiny mountainside chapel in Colorado. Friends had lent us their condo for the week, and my parents wanted their second marriage to be as private as possible. Just us, a pastor and a church, and a new beginning.

A clear, spring-fed stream ran right by the chapel, and we took pictures beforehand next to the spring's river rocks. Brittany and I wore matching lace dresses, but that was the last thing on our minds. The sun was shining brightly that day, crisp and cool for October, and as we entered the chapel, the sun streamed through the stained glass windows at the front of the church. The beams of light were distinct, like rainbow-colored lines shining down on us. I felt glorious, like I was in another world.

Brittany played the piano for the ceremony, bawling the whole stately way through Pachelbel's "Canon in D." I kept my emotions tightly wrapped. Mom was crying. Dad was crying. Somebody in our family had to keep it together.

But I was happy.

Ecstatic was more like it. The darkest part of the night was over at last. God had finally answered our far-fetched request in a way we once could only dream about. Mom and Dad were together again. The dawn had arrived, and from here on out I knew everything in our family was going to be absolutely perfect.

CHAPTER 9

Discovery

Cheryl

The question came out of nowhere, stunning me as if I'd been slapped in the face.

It came two years after Jeff and I had remarried, when the girls were in eighth grade. I'd just pulled to the curb to pick them up from middle school. The question burst from my daughter Brittany as she closed the car door and strapped on her seat belt in the front seat.

Lauren had bounded into the backseat, her eyes in the rearview mirror round with disbelief. They'd obviously been talking while waiting on the school's front lawn before I drove up. Comparing notes. Two thirteen-year-olds figuring out how to get to the bottom of things.

"Mom, did you have an affair?" Brittany asked again.

"I heard you the first time," I said slowly. The girls were both belted in now, but my foot was still on the brake, the car idling at the curb.

"Rebecca said something to me," Brittany said, with an attitude of junior high nonchalance. "We were just hanging out by our lockers between classes. Isn't that weird she'd ever think something like that? I figured we'd better ask you about it."

It isn't unusual for the question of infidelity to be raised when there's been a divorce. But I'd always figured I'd field this question with my daughters when they were older. Maybe in college, when they could better handle the topic. Or maybe when they were in their twenties or thirties and had husbands of their own. That's when I'd always imagined the conversation taking place. Always later. Much later.

I swallowed. "Yes," I said softly.

I said the word in answer to Brittany's question. And then I started to cry.

The girls sat in stunned silence. I shifted the car into drive and headed home. By the time we reached our driveway, I was bawling. Nothing more was said until I shifted into park and turned off the ignition. None of us made a move to climb out. I cracked a window to get some fresh air and tried to dry my eyes. There in the car I started to unravel the story. I began by saying, "If you're angry with me, I completely understand."

Two years into my marriage I'd begun to feel alone. That's a difficult concept to convey to your daughters, particularly when you're now remarried to their father, who has always been a shining knight in their eyes—and who has done a ton of growing since you were first married. Jeff and I both had been growing. I tried to explain the concept of loneliness in a marriage as best as I knew how.

My problems in marriage had started because Jeff and I were two people who had our eyes on the wrong goals. We were young and ambitious, eager to climb career ladders and live the good life. We had no idea that a healthy marriage is built on communication, unconditional love, and a solid biblical foundation. When it came to marrying Jeff, I was the starry-eyed girl who'd always dreamed of finding her very own Brad Pitt, or whoever the Hollywood hunk of the day was. When Jeff first came into my world, he was all that—the absolute man of my dreams. But as our marriage progressed, I found that Jeff wasn't as flawless as I'd first imagined him to be. For example, when we went bike riding, for him the activity was all about reaching a destination. For me, bike riding meant a chance to talk and connect as a couple. In my mind, the problems were all one-sided. My husband wasn't giving me what I longed for.

Time went by, and I felt increasingly alone. I was desperately afraid our life together would continue to be imperfect, but I had no idea how to communicate any of my deepest thoughts to my husband. So I buried my fears. I stuffed them down deep and hoped they'd go away.

For six years I didn't do anything about my feelings. I just kept stuffing them down. The girls were born, and everything in my life took a beautiful turn. But even then, I still felt this strange sense of incompleteness.

In March 1990, eight years into my marriage—when the girls were not yet two—the company I worked for sent me to Florida on a sales trip. There, I met with a colleague named Todd. He worked from a different office in a different city, and our conversations began innocently enough. He shared some of the struggles he was having in his marriage, and for the first time I shared some of the struggles I was having in mine. At the end of that trip, when Jeff and the girls picked me up at the airport and Jeff hugged me, it dawned on me that when I was away I hadn't missed my husband at all.

My colleague and I went back to our respective offices in our respective cities, but we began talking for hours on the phone each day. I never suspected things would go further than just talk. For goodness' sake—he was a married man and twenty years older than me. But the downward slope was already greased. Just one month later Todd flew from where he lived in northern California to where I lived in southern California. We met at a hotel, and that day our relationship turned into a full-blown adulterous affair.

I never told anyone. Not a soul. My actions that day weren't like me, I rationalized. I would never cheat on my husband. I was a good girl. A Catholic. I convinced myself that I'd just made a momentary mistake—that was all. A big mistake, sure, but no one ever needed to know. That's why when Jeff's company transferred us to Dallas, I felt so relieved. I could put this mistake behind me. My secret would stay safe with me forever.

Jeff and the girls and I moved to Dallas, and for a short time everything was okay. But I deeply missed the emotional connection I'd developed with Todd. We began talking on the phone again every day. That pull began to lead me further down the hazardous path I'd started on.

Sure, I'd started to go to church by then. Something was tugging on my soul, even though at the time I didn't know what it was. The problem was that I'd so hardened my heart to Jeff that the change I'd begun to experience with God wasn't entering my marriage yet. I'd convinced myself that I was finished with my marriage. I believed I was deeply in love with someone else. So I progressed down the divorce road, and, yes, the way I handled the divorce was absolutely wrong. Having the sheriff serve papers to Jeff at our home was another indication of my inability to communicate. I didn't know how to tell anybody how I actually felt deep inside—not even my husband. That's why I filed the papers secretly. I was petrified to tell Jeff I wanted a divorce. So, unfortunately, he was absolutely blindsided by the news. There are so many things I wish I could do over in my life. How I acted with Jeff was simply horrible.

I thought things would be so much better after the divorce, but they weren't. Todd and I started making plans to live in the same city, to get married someday. He flew out to see me, and I flew out to see him. The girls met him. He even came to their school. He would never take the place of their father, and I didn't want him to. I just wanted him all for me. But I quickly began to realize that Todd wasn't fulfilling the deepest desires of my heart. Not really.

The thing that began to save me was something beyond myself. I had never studied the Bible before, and I was curious and intrigued. At my new church, I was around people who were continually kind to me, offering me grace, forgiveness, and compassion, even though my life was a mess. This was new to me. I hadn't done anything to deserve these people's kindness, and yet there it was. Each Sunday I couldn't wait to be at church. Three months after the divorce was final, I came to know Christ as my personal Savior. As great as that day was, it was also devastating because I could see clearly the wrongness of what I'd done. God had saved me, but there were still huge pieces of my life to mend. I'd left a crumbled marriage and fractured family in the wake of my selfishness.

Jeff began to grow spiritually too. In our early years of marriage, we had gone to church only on Christmas and Easter. But during the time surrounding the divorce, even though he had a ton of questions, Jeff ran back to the Lord. He didn't know why God would allow something so bad to happen to our family. At first Jeff couldn't understand how he'd played a part in the marriage's collapse, although a smaller part than mine. Still, he was willing to change and be open to God's plan.

In addition to Jeff's role as a sponsor of the high school youth group, he began attending a large men's Bible study held weekly at the church. There, he listened to men he respected—articulate, intelligent men who spoke Jeff's language. They clearly taught the Word of God. Jeff began to understand that there is a deeper purpose to life than simply advancing in a career or acquiring a lot of possessions.

One morning in the fall of 1992, about three months after our divorce was final, I was reading my Bible and the voice of God began to whisper to me. That's the only way I can describe it. It wasn't an audible voice, but a distinct and powerful sense that God's will was being revealed to me. God was telling me that I needed to pursue reconciliation with Jeff. After two months of wrestling over this prompting, I finally called Jeff and asked if I could come over to talk to him.

Jeff reluctantly agreed. At the end of our conversation, I told Jeff I'd become a Christian, and I believed God wanted us to reconcile our marriage. Jeff was crying, but it wasn't out of sympathy. It was out of pain and anger. He was the one who'd insisted we go for counseling, even when I'd clammed up. He'd wanted to keep the marriage together all along. He was the one who'd been served divorce papers by the sheriff. Jeff couldn't even look me in the eye. He asked me to leave.

I drove home, sat in my chair, and concluded that I'd misunderstood God's voice. I figured that if Jeff didn't want anything to do with me anymore, I should just get on with my life. What I didn't realize was that God wanted me to persevere with him in prayer. God had a plan for my life, and I needed to endure with him through this time of uncertainty and not try to go down my own path. That meant waiting.

I wasn't very good at waiting.

Especially when the waiting turned into years. Jeff and I continued to experience a good working relationship when it came to parenting, but that was all. In the meantime, he was growing in his faith, and I was growing in mine. I'd read verses like Ephesians 3:20, about how God can do immeasurably more than we dare ask or think, and I'd still dream of Jeff and me getting back together someday. But I knew it would take a miracle.

Jeff was lonely. He'd been praying that God would bring a godly woman into his life. He shared his prayer request one morning in his men's Bible study, and the men prayed for Jeff on and off for months. Finally one of them said to Jeff, "Did you ever consider that maybe the woman we've been praying for all along is your ex-wife?"

One night Jeff read Proverbs 3:5-6, a passage he'd memorized as a child. "Trust in the LORD with all your heart, and do not lean on your own understanding. In all your ways acknowledge him, and he will make straight your paths." A lightbulb clicked on in Jeff's head. He decided to do exactly as the passage said—to trust in God fully. That night Jeff rededicated his life to God.

Once Jeff and I landed on the same page spiritually, things began to take off. I guess you could say we started dating as a family. We certainly appeared on each other's doorsteps a lot. God was pulling us back together with new speed. When it came to my ex-husband and me, our lives were completely different now. We weren't controlled by the same selfish desires anymore. We both wanted what was best for each other. But one huge question needed to be answered.

When the girls were gone at summer camp, Jeff and I did some serious talking and praying together. We talked about getting remarried, but Jeff asked the last huge question—and it was a good one. "Cheryl, how do I know you're not going to do the same thing again?"

I sat for a moment, praying silently, wondering what to say. *Lord, I don't know how to promise another human I'm never going to fail him again.* But in that moment I knew the answer. God was central to both our lives now. It was the truth. "This is not really about you and me anymore," I said. "It's about God now, and I never want to disappoint my God again."

The rest is history.

That's what I told my daughters, there in the car in front of the house, on the afternoon when I picked them up at middle school. Yes, I'd had an affair. And, yes, I was sorry. So extremely sorry. And, yes, God had wondrously, miraculously made all things new.

When I finished my story, I looked at my daughters, still through tears, and asked them what they thought about all this. To tell my complete story to my children, to admit to them I'd done things I felt very ashamed about, was at the top of the list of the hardest things I'd ever done.

Lauren stayed quiet in the backseat. I think she was still taking it all in.

Brittany spoke first. She spoke for herself and for her sister, as she had always done. "Mom, God has forgiven you. Dad has forgiven you. And we forgive you too."

Lauren nodded and smiled.

God had brought about this day for a reason. It was such a difficult thing to tell the girls my story, yet I also felt happy that I didn't need to carry the weight for another ten years or longer. God had brought us all back together, and now he'd brought about a new level of honesty. The secret was out. We were truly a team again.

XO

Years later when the girls were in the early years of college, I was upstairs one night in Brittany's room, hanging out with both girls. We were talking about something different, but for some reason my mind went back to the maturity of my daughters' response that day in our driveway when they were both in junior high. Neither of the girls had gotten mad at me. Neither had shouted or stomped her feet or called me names, although they had every right to do so. They were filled with such graciousness and forgiveness, even as children. What they had said amazed me, and I wondered, *Will they ever understand the priceless gift they gave me?* It was still beyond my comprehension.

That night in Brittany's room we were talking about Casey, a friend of theirs. She was the same age as the twins. Casey had experienced a much harder life, and we discussed our wonderment that she had traversed her experiences with such grace and strength.

Casey's father had suffered a sudden heart attack and died when the girls were seniors in high school. I'd known her family. We all had. They were genuine, joyful people, high-octane types, and full of love as a family. This girl was extremely close to her dad, and seeing him die became for my girls one of the first seasons of suffering they had ever encountered on someone else's behalf.

Casey's family limped along without their father. Some days at high school, my girls told me, were very hard for Casey. She could be abrupt when she was around her friends, and she didn't act like that normally. This girl was grieving deeply, letting the sorrow flow out of her.

Then, two years after her father died, another heartache struck. When it rained hardship on this family, it poured. Casey's little brother Cody was diagnosed with a rare and aggressive form of cancer. The disease formed a grapefruit-size tumor on Cody's tailbone. He battled through chemo and radiation treatments, and for some time nobody knew if he would live or die.

This time, however, Casey navigated her family's suffering with a new stance of determination.

I asked my daughters how Casey was able to do that. I was working to form an answer in the back of my mind, but I wanted to see how they might answer the question first. I thought about how life throws curveballs at everyone. Bad experiences happen to us all. Sometimes we bring about our own heartache—like I had done with my divorce. Other times the heartache is thrust upon us—like Casey's dad dying and her brother getting sick.

Brittany spoke first again. The words tumbled out of her. "Casey told us there were moments of such huge pain that she just wanted to lie down and die. But because of her faith, she decided that no matter how miserable she felt, she wasn't going to crumble under the weight of all the hardship that hit her. She vowed to keep going forward."

Lauren looked up from the big, round, comfy chair in the corner of the room and brushed back a strand of hair. None of us knew it then, but a few years later her propeller accident would take place, and she would face a similar temptation to crumble under life's hardships. I could see she was chewing on something big, perhaps a truth that had long existed deep within her character but had never surfaced before.

"That's what courage looks like, Mom," Lauren said, after she had thought awhile. "Even when life hits you hard, you keep on going."

CHAPTER 10

The Beginning of a Calling

Lauren

Carter and I were dating.

Well, not for real.

I mean, Carter was the cutest guy in ninth grade, and we texted each other back and forth in the hallways at church youth group when we were both fourteen. We would tease each other about grades and the stinky sandwiches we brought to lunch at school and the crazy color of each other's shirts. Some girls whispered how Carter and I were *totally* in love together forever, but I laughed at the idea. It was all just silly fun.

I met Carter at church. To be honest, I kind of hoped he would ask me out for real because he was a twin just like me and had a sly sense of humor, which always makes for a good friend. But I wasn't going to do the asking. I doodled Carter's initials next to mine on the front cover of my notebook at school, and we even went to a dance together once. Before the dance my mom called his mom, Sharon, and they compared notes like good mothers do. Mom saw right away where Carter got his kindness and quick sense of humor. My mom and Carter's mom became lasting friends.

That's how it went in early high school for me. The days were filled with innocent fun. Family life settled into that good routine of normalcy and security. Mom and Dad were together again. There were no more big secrets. Brittany and I dug into our schoolwork and played softball and practiced the piano and went to art classes and had crushes on guys and dreamed of the future—that was the extent of our world.

After school and on weekends, we hung out with a big group of girl-friends—Rebecca, Casey, Tiffany, McKenzie, and Caroline. We also got along well with a bunch of guys from our church youth group, and we would play "keep-away" wars with them. Somebody would steal somebody else's hat and hide it, and then some guy would make a video showing the hat in different places all over town. We'd go to the park and play capture the flag at dusk, yelling and whooping as we ran around. Tiffany lived next to the golf course, and on weekends all the girls would end up at her house for sleepovers. We'd rent a funny chick flick and make dinner and play flashlight tag on the golf course. There was some girl-drama, but not much. We had a lot of wholesome fun together, and we created most of it ourselves. We weren't wrapped up in any of the darker trappings of high school—drugs, alcohol, wild parties.

Of course, we cared about clothes. It's a rule for teen girls. We even got competitive about it, which is easy to do, especially at that age. But the ultimate goal was for each girl to find her individual sense of style. Brittany and I weren't wearing OshKosh anymore, like Dad used to get for us as kids. So that meant we needed to figure out how best to present ourselves to the world. I developed a passion for the style of clothes at Urban Outfitters, a store filled with racks of creative, organic-looking designs—hippieish stuff like cute-patterned tops, cool jeans, flats and wedges, a style that's almost bohemian. Brittany's style became more closely aligned with the store Anthropologie. She liked fitted clothes with empire waists—a more polished look than mine.

Our growth involved much more than clothes. Mom and Dad wanted to expand our horizons beyond Plano during those growing-up years, so during breaks from school they took us on trips around the country, and even on some international trips. We went to North

Carolina, Colorado, San Francisco, New York, Greece, the Bahamas, and Canada. We visited relatives in Georgia, Ohio, and West Virginia, and quickly saw that not all of America grows up like we did in Plano.

"Plano is a bubble," our parents told us more than once, and over time we learned what that meant. In West Plano it's normal to receive a brand-new car for your sixteenth birthday present—and plenty of kids are bummed that their BMW isn't the precise shade of red they wanted.

But that's not how it was in our family. Our parents didn't give us everything we wanted. We did chores around the house and worked in restaurants and at clothing stores to earn spending money. In eighth grade we began to volunteer at a community outreach program called H.I.S. BridgeBuilders in a not-so-affluent part of Dallas. We hung around with the younger children who lived there, playing games and doing crafts with them. It all helped shape a larger view of the world for us. "If you've been given much, then much is required of you," Dad said to us more than once, paraphrasing Jesus' words.[2] It was a lesson we never forgot.

XO

A lot of our friends started going to Prestonwood, a private Christian school down the road, and we transferred there at the start of our junior year. We wore uniforms at Prestonwood—pleated plaid navy-and-dark-green skirts, blue or white polo or oxford shirts, navy sweater-vests. Brittany and I didn't mind the uniforms. We never had to think about what we were going to wear in the morning. Sometimes we didn't even change when we got home from school because the uniforms were so comfy.

During spring break our junior year, our Spanish teacher arranged for students to travel to Cuba for extra language study. Brittany and I had grown up speaking a lot of Spanish, and the trip sounded like a real adventure—you couldn't even get to the country directly from America. You had to fly to Mexico first and then enter Cuba. Mom and Dad came along as chaperones, which we didn't mind. Once there, we were put into groups of four along with a national host, and we traveled out to the countryside to meet with people in their villages, speak the language, and talk to them about whatever was on their minds.

Mom, Dad, Brittany, and I were put in the same group, and everybody we met was superfriendly. Even though most of the people we encountered were extremely poor, they'd bring out coffee or tea or some food for us to eat. They'd invite us into their homes and tell us about the difficulties of living in a Communist country. There was no freedom of religion in Cuba, but everybody seemed to believe in something anyway. Some of the houses contained demonic-looking sculptures, images that the people worshiped, they told us. Some people were into Santeria, a mix of ancient African spiritism with some Catholicism thrown in. They asked what we believed, and we talked about Jesus. Nobody seemed to mind. Mom and Dad told the story of the split in their marriage being healed—a story that translated well in any culture.

One afternoon our interpreter invited us to his home in a little sugar mill town. In his yard was a huge pig. I thought about how great it would be to have your very own pig for a pet and asked what its name was, but our guide quickly made it clear that this was no pet. It was earmarked for dinner sometime soon. He took us on a tour of his house—two rooms total—and even showed us his closet. One lonely pair of pants swung next to a threadbare jacket. That was it. Those were all the clothes he owned. It was a real eye-opener to realize that plenty of people around the world live in similar ways. Before we returned to America, Dad emptied his suitcase and gave the man all the clothes he had with him.

The people who sponsored us in Cuba were Christians, and we were surprised to learn the depth of their faith. One day they looked tired. When we asked why, they told us they had been up until four that morning praying for us. It felt very humbling to receive that kind of blessing from them.

As it turned out, we had a reason to be extra glad they were praying. That same night we headed back to our hotel later than usual. We'd been driving in a little rental car—not one of those chrome-grilled 1950s American models you see driving around in Havana in the movies, but a tiny little compact—absolutely bare-bones transportation with a stick shift. Neither of my parents was used to driving a stick, so they'd been popping the clutch and stalling the car throughout the day. Brittany and I gritted our teeth in the backseat.

That night we were driving on a country highway and stopped quickly before making a left turn. The car stalled before we'd completed the turn, stranding us in front of oncoming traffic. Cars honked and swerved around us. Some drivers raised their fists. My parents frantically tried to start the car. I looked up and saw a huge truck, fully loaded, barreling straight toward us. The driver was traveling at highway speeds, and there was no way he was going to be able to stop or swerve quickly enough. "Mo-o-o-o-o-o-m!" I yelled from the backseat.

Suddenly we felt something push the car forward. We cleared the lane just as the truck whooshed past us, its horn blaring. We thought another car had hit us from behind, but when we turned around to look, no one was there. There wasn't another car in sight. Our car's engine still hadn't started. To this day, we have no idea what shoved our car forward.

After our adventures in Cuba, it was a relief to be back home. As we got older, we came to appreciate Prestonwood more and more. Almost all the kids who went there were serious about their studies. We immersed ourselves in chemistry, Spanish, history, Advanced Placement English, and Advanced Placement calculus. Calculus was probably my favorite class, simply because I loved our teacher so much. She was one of those highly dedicated, inspiring instructors that Hollywood should make a movie about. Brittany and I would go to her classroom during our free period and study calculus more just so we could be around her. I made a mental note to dedicate myself completely to my calling, whatever that was going to be someday, based on her example.

At this point, I had no idea what I wanted to do for a career. Not an inkling. When I was a little kid, I'd dreamed of being a veterinarian because I loved animals so much. In high school, in addition to math, I loved anything creative—photography, fashion, and art. I didn't like writing as much, even though the career aptitude test I took in twelfth grade indicated I should be a journalist. I certainly never loved writing in high school the way some kids do. I was more interested in style, color, and unique portrayals of people's personalities.

Our graduating class consisted of eighty-eight students. Brittany finished second in our class academically and was the salutatorian. I finished eleventh, which I felt pretty proud of, although I knew I could have done better. Brittany stressed about grades, but I was more carefree. Grades mattered to me, and I was competitive in my own way, but I just didn't worry much about grades like Brittany did. I had other things on my mind.

Much of what was on my mind centered around a football player named Tim. He was a year older than me and was good friends with Carter, my other close guy friend. At the end of his junior year, Tim asked Carter, "Would you mind if I asked Lauren to prom?" Carter said sure, so Tim asked me. I would have gone with Carter if he'd asked first, but he wasn't making any moves. Tim played quarterback for our football team and was six feet tall with blue eyes and blond, slightly long, curly hair—a real *Friday Night Lights* type of guy.

At first, we just did a lot of talking; we were not officially dating. Then Tim was playing in an away game and got tackled head-on. He went to the ER that night with broken vertebrae in his back and was in a brace for months afterward. He never played football again. While Tim recovered, we hung out more. Soon we started spending so much time together that it felt natural to consider ourselves a couple. He was smart, funny, generous, and sociable—even when dealing with his painful injury. As he began to improve, we started going on more real dates.

We were never the type of couple who always obsessively hangs around each other, and we both liked that fact. It was a fun-loving, friendly relationship, a great introduction to the world of dating. We kissed and held hands, but that was the extent of our physical relationship. Brittany was happy for us; there was never any jealousy on her part. Tim and I dated all through my junior year and his senior year. When Tim graduated, he went to the University of Oklahoma, about three and half hours away, and for a while we committed to keep dating long distance.

I graduated high school in 2006 and attended Texas A&M University the next fall, along with Brittany. I couldn't tell you exactly why we

ABOVE ▲

As always, in our
OshKosh B'gosh outfits

LEFT ◄

Our first Christmas:
Brittany (left) and me (right)

ABOVE ▲

Playing with makeup
at Christmas

My all-time favorite photo of Britt and me

Obviously, I was destined for a career in fashion!

XOXOXOXOXOXOXOXOXOXOXOXOXOXOXOXOXOXOX

BELOW ▼
At the golf course my grandparents own . . .
We learned how to play early!

RIGHT ▶
Fun at the lake!

So many family pictures from Britt's and my childhood show our parents apart. As hard as it was to spend time with Mom and Dad separately, I'm grateful we always knew how much they loved us. . . .

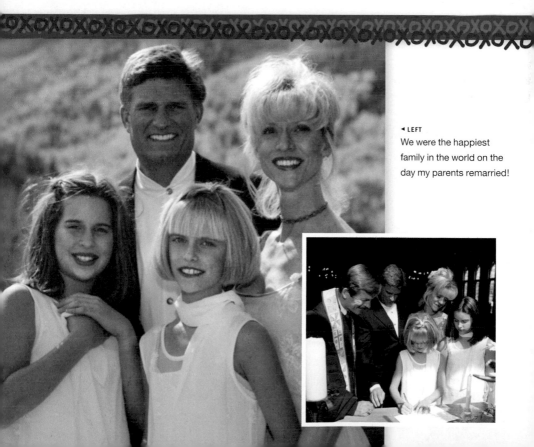

◀ LEFT
We were the happiest family in the world on the day my parents remarried!

Special Moments

ABOVE ▲

Getting ready to ski at the lake

ABOVE ▲

Our first football game at Texas A&M

My life in New York City was even more special when I could share it with Britt, Mom, and Dad (who, as usual, was behind the camera).

Graduation day! I was so excited for whatever my future would hold.

BELOW ▼

I love spending time with my extended family—aunts, uncles, cousins. This is me with my cousin Mimi, who is a precious gift to all of us.

ABOVE ▲

My beautiful sister and her handsome husband absolutely shone on their wedding day.

This was the first vacation we took together (to Savannah, Georgia) after Shaun became part of the family. We all loved having him there, but my dad was especially happy to have another guy on the trip!

BELOW ▼

One of our friends was doing a photography workshop, and we volunteered to come in and help. I love this photo she caught of Mom and me doing what we do so often—laughing, enjoying each other's company, and just being close.

ABOVE ▲

My dad is always there for me. Whether he's listening and giving advice, or going on a fun, spontaneous adventure with me, we make such special memories together. I have so much respect for how he has led our family through the toughest times. This is us at a banquet for Prestonwood Christian Academy.

The plane I was in the night my life changed

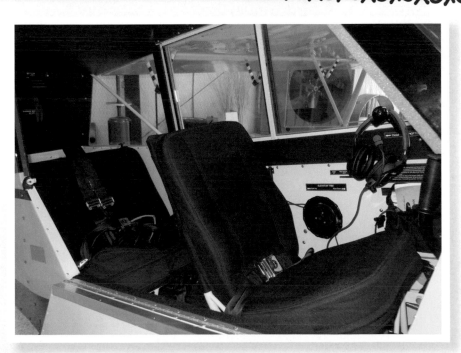

Close-up of the two-seat interior

On March 7, just a few months after the accident, family friends put together an unforgettable night called the LoLo Event. We had no idea about most of the details ahead of time. We just showed up—and walked into a world beyond anything we could have imagined.

I had missed Fashion Week while I was recovering, so they brought it to me. The runway was made of pink sand; the models wore beautiful clothes from my favorite stores. And all the proceeds raised went to help with my medical bills.

Since the accident, I had hardly seen anyone other than family. I can't describe how it felt to have so many people come together that night to show me and my family how much they loved us.

picked that school. Some of our friends were heading there, and it was a good school academically with a lot of fun traditions. Both of us were General Studies majors at first—the equivalent of being "undecided."

Texas A&M is located in College Station, about three and a half hours from our house, so we moved into a dorm on campus. The dorms were okay, coed but not wild, and mostly everybody did their own thing. We hung out with the friends we knew from back home.

Off-campus, it was more of a crazy environment, but even then not in a bad way. We went to all the football games and chanted along with the crowd. Everything with the Aggies is extremely spirited and rooted in long-standing collegiate traditions. We learned to do the drills pretty fast or else. During the games you put your hands up and shout "Woop!" really loudly. If you're a freshman you point your hands one way, and if you're a senior you point another way—and if any freshmen get caught doing the senior move, they'll be punished. Everything is just silly and fun, and everybody says "howdy" and "Gig 'em Aggies!" I had a blast with that part of school life.

We discovered an awesome Wednesday night Bible study on campus that met in the basketball arena. Hundreds of students attended, and all these amazing speakers came in to encourage and challenge us, which was cool.

But sometimes I felt like I didn't fit in at Texas A&M, and that feeling happened more and more often.

It took awhile to grapple with that feeling and even articulate it to myself. I began thinking through my life so far—what I liked and didn't like, who I was and what I gravitated toward—and concluded I was more of an offbeat type of personality, while Texas A&M is more of an "onbeat" type of school. It's like a tone or style or way of seeing the world. To me, *onbeat* describes a traditional, expected, staid, and predictable approach to life. *Offbeat* is quirky, unconventional, unexpected, and diverse.

I didn't show my offbeat side very much. But as the months at Texas A&M passed, I began to realize that it wasn't my calling to stay at that school. As a middle-class church girl in Texas, I was expected to go to college, get married quickly, work at a job for short time, then settle down into child rearing. I wasn't against any of those things, but it just didn't feel like a direction I was going to head anytime soon.

One afternoon at Texas A&M, Brittany and I got into an argument. I don't even remember what it was about. Arguments are rare for us, but once the heat died down and we both went to our own corners to cool off, the argument became the catalyst for me to do some serious soul-searching.

In high school I'd read the book *Roaring Lambs* by the late Bob Briner, an Emmy Award–winning television producer. He writes about being an authentic Christian wherever you are and encourages young people to go into industries that Christians traditionally don't enter. When I was growing up in Sunday school, the expectation was that if you wanted to live for God, you'd end up being a missionary or pastor's wife or working for a Christian organization—something like that. That was fine for people who were led that way, but it just wasn't me. Briner says that God purposely places passions in our hearts and doesn't intend for us all to end up in the same locations or careers. God wants us to be excellent in whatever we do for the sake of his glory. He wants us to use our unique gifts and talents to be influential in every walk of life.

I felt as if I could relate with that open-ended direction much more than the traditional approach. I began to feel a specific nudge to the fashion world or maybe art. I knew I'd need more training and should probably attend a university in New York City. I had no idea about any of the specifics of the calling. But I knew that this rough day at Texas A&M signaled the beginning of the end for me there. Brittany and I patched things up quickly, and she expressed her support for anything I wanted to do. I called my mom later that night and told her what I was feeling. She said to step forward courageously. A day later I called Dana Crawford, my mom's good friend, and she counseled me to do the same thing—go where God was leading me, wherever that might be.

At the end of that semester, I left Texas A&M for good. Brittany wasn't positive she should stay there either, but she decided to stick it out until the end of the year. I attended community college near home that spring semester. Tim and I broke up sometime around then as well. Clearly, my life would be moving in a new direction, though I didn't know where I was headed just then.

XO

That next fall I still didn't know what I was supposed to be doing. I enrolled at community college again and kept chipping away at general education courses. I figured that it's wise to do the next most obvious thing, even when the future remains unclear.

About that time my mom started talking to me about taking a research trip to New York. Dana was going to come along. Her son, Chace, is three years older than me, and he had recently begun working as one of the lead characters on a new TV show called *Gossip Girl*, which was being filmed in New York. His mom told me about meeting Eric Daman, the wardrobe guy there. "Eric is great," Dana said. "Very positive and creative. You could learn a lot from working at a place like that."

That November my mom, Dana, and I flew to New York City. We'd set up several tours at art schools and universities that offered majors in photography, art, and fashion, but the trip didn't have a specific agenda. It was mostly to explore the landscape and determine what the next step for me might be.

I'd been to New York before with my family. It's always exciting to fly into JFK Airport, catch a cab, and see the big city. Right when we landed, Dana called Chace to tell him we'd arrived. He said he had a fitting with Eric Daman that same afternoon and invited us to come over and say hello. A fitting doesn't happen every day—it's more like a once-a-week thing—so we knew we'd lucked out to arrive on a day when Chace would be meeting with Eric.

We went to the production studios and met Eric's assistant, Sami, and toured the wardrobe department at *Gossip Girl*. She's naturally pretty with long brown hair, which she wears up most of the time. Sami proved to be instantly approachable and down-to-earth.

I had this image in mind that the wardrobe department of a TV show would be luxurious and glamorous, with lots of high-profile celebrities walking in and out. But it wasn't like that at all. In the fall of 2007, *Gossip Girl* was just getting started, and most of the actors were pretty much unknown then. The people I met that day were all very professional but still very normal. They were passionate, driven, and artistic— and yet just the same type of people you'd meet up with in a coffee shop. I quickly felt very comfortable around them.

Eric Daman was carrying on with his normal workday. He had all these magazine pictures taped up in the wardrobe room that inspired each character's look for the show. Chace explained that it was fairly rare to run into Eric like this but told us not to worry. He introduced us, and we started talking. Eric Daman was totally cool. There wasn't any plan to our conversation. It wasn't even a meeting. It was more just hanging out, getting a tour of the set.

On her own initiative, Dana asked, "Eric, do you ever do internships here?" (We hadn't talked about this before among ourselves.)

"No," Eric said, then turned to me. "We never have before. But I think we'd be up for it if you could arrange it through your college."

I just smiled and said, "Wow, okay." And the conversation was over, as quick as that.

Mom, Dana, and I went out to dinner that night at a Cuban fusion restaurant in the heart of the city. We dined on lightly seared tuna and delicious crunchy salads with soy-lime vinaigrette. While we ate, we talked about the university tours lined up for the next day.

"You know, Lo," Mom said, putting down her fork. "I think you should consider pursuing an internship at *Gossip Girl.*"

Dana agreed. "It might be a bit uncomfortable to leave your home and family and come to the big city all by yourself, but I know you could handle it."

I took another sip of water and thought, *You know, I think I would really like that.* But it all seemed so improbable. So out of the norm for me. How could a specific calling to the world of fashion begin to take wings all because of a random meeting with Eric Daman and a quick question about internships?

Surely God was working behind the scenes, leading me forward to a new, unknown world waiting to be discovered. I couldn't explain it any other way.

CHAPTER 11

New York City

Lauren

In early January 2008, I flew to New York City to begin an internship in the wardrobe department at *Gossip Girl*. I was nineteen years old and ready to be on my own in the city for four and a half months. True, it was a big step for me with a lot of unknowns, but I also felt peace about this next season of life. Mom, Dad, and Brittany all flew out with me to help me get settled. Fear was the furthest thing from my mind. When the plane touched down, I almost laughed out loud. Taking this journey into unfamiliar territory was exactly what I wanted to do.

There was only one problem. A big problem. We landed smack-dab in the middle of a writers' strike, and production of *Gossip Girl* shut down. Tons of other shows throughout the industry were in the same predicament.

We had known about the strike beforehand. It had started a few weeks earlier, but everybody in the industry was confident the strike would be over soon. Some of the unscripted and reality shows were still running, and some shows had all their writing completed for the season before the strike began.[3] So I was confident that even if my internship on *Gossip Girl* were delayed, I could still make a lot of good contacts and land a position somewhere else in the industry. All I needed to do was get to the city.

I'd arranged to rent an apartment with two other girls in a complex owned by The King's College. Our apartment was located in midtown Manhattan on Thirty-Fourth and Sixth, right next to the Empire State Building. One of my roommates, Lindsay, was a friend from high school. Our other roommate, Kristin, was new to both of us and had been assigned to us by the college. Both girls were also doing internships—one at NBC and the other with a public relations company.

I was the first to arrive at the apartment and unfasten the heavy locks. The door swung open, and I peeked inside. I'd heard stories of New York apartments being small, and ours was no exception. There was a living area, a kitchen, a bathroom, and another room, but the entire unit was about the size of a master bathroom in Dallas. I chuckled when I looked out the window. It had sounded glamorous to hear that our new home was located in the heart of the city, but our building was sandwiched between two other buildings. The view out the window showed a tiny sliver of Thirty-Fourth Street and two brick walls. I could hear traffic, sirens, horns, people walking by. We were most definitely not in Kansas anymore, Toto.

I'm sort of a neat freak, and the first thing I wanted to do was clean. The apartment was tidy, but it smelled different from anything I'd ever experienced in Dallas—older, musty, like a lot of people had lived there before. While Dad went to find a hardware store to get a part we needed for the sink, Mom, Brittany, and I stayed and did some deep cleaning. We turned up the music and danced around. It was fun to have them there. My family was set to return home the next day. That night we all went to a hotel together. The next morning they hugged me good-bye and flew home. My roommates would be arriving the following day, so that night I stayed in my apartment—alone—for the very first time.

Around midnight I went to bed. I opened the window and gazed outside at my new view of the brick walls. A dumpster opened and closed somewhere below. I shivered from a chill and closed the window. I wasn't afraid. Some furniture had been delivered—two desks and a couch. I'd shipped my sheets because it was cheaper that way. They hadn't arrived yet, so I lay down on the couch and pulled a blanket over me. I could still hear the traffic of the city. Horns. Sirens. I was here. Truly here. A huge sense of excitement crept over me. *God, thank you so much for this first night in New York*, I prayed. *I can't wait for whatever happens next.*

It was good to have Kristin and Lindsay move in. Lindsay is pretty, with brown hair and blondish highlights. Kristin, the girl I hadn't known before, was from Rochester, and I sensed we'd become close friends. Kristin is short and cute, with dark brown hair. We all hit it off well. The day after that, both their internships started, and they left for work.

But me?

Oh boy, I thought. *I need to get a job.*

I had e-mailed Sami, Eric Daman's assistant at *Gossip Girl*, several times already. Sami was confident the strike would end quickly. She promised to contact me immediately whenever word came, but so far all was silent. Yet I didn't worry. I had no doubt that God had led me to New York, so I didn't doubt that God would provide another job in his time and way.

XO

That same afternoon I was walking around Rockefeller Center by myself when I took a good look around me. The Center was about fifteen or sixteen blocks from our apartment. All around me skyscrapers towered—the huge GE Building, Radio City Music Hall, the Time-Life Building, stores, shops, restaurants, offices, apartments. The crowds on the sidewalk moved quickly. People looked grittier than they did in Dallas. Everybody was well dressed and fine featured but more natural looking than back home, wearing less makeup. I wore heeled boots over my jeans, a cute top, and a faux-fur jacket. I felt funky and hip, and I wasn't nervous at all. The fast pace energized me. *God*, I prayed, *if it's not* Gossip Girl, *then where do you want me?*

Right then, a voice in the back of my mind said, *Call Lindsey again.*

This wasn't Lindsay O., my apartment roommate, but Lindsey R., a girl a few years older than me who knew our family from when my dad worked with the youth group years ago. This Lindsey had always been like a big sister to me, and I knew she worked in New York. I'd called her a few weeks earlier to ask about the industry, but she'd never called back. Calling her again seemed kind of silly, but I felt a new sense of confidence being in New York all by myself.

"Lauren Scruggs!" she said, her voice in a rush. "Oh, it's so good to hear from you. You're at the top of my list to call. I've been traveling, and it's been a crazy last couple of months. What are you doing, anyway?"

I explained my situation. She knew all about the writers' strike.

Lindsey paused, like she was thinking hard. "Lauren, have you ever heard of Michael Kors?"

I smiled. "*The* Michael Kors? Sure—I love what he does."

"I'm working for his showroom now in the women's division. Why don't you intern here? You could start right away, and if the writers' strike ends, you could leave anytime and go back to *Gossip Girl.*"

I couldn't believe my ears. Just like that—an opening!

Two days later I started work as an intern at the design studios of Michael Kors. That first morning I walked to the check-in desk inside the showroom and couldn't believe my eyes. A designer's personality is reflected in a building. Michael Kors is known for doing amazing things with neutral colors (camel is his favorite), so everything was painted camel and white. Tall, leggy models were walking in and out of the building. A huge TV was showing a Michael Kors fashion show from the previous season. Everything was beautiful, inspiring, and completely incredible.

Michael Kors is one of New York's top clothing designers. He creates women's and men's clothing, women's handbags, shoes, and other accessories. He has full collection boutiques in New York, Beverly Hills, Palm Beach, Manhasset, and Chicago. Celebrities who've worn Michael Kors's designs include everybody from Michelle Obama to Jennifer Garner. I'd seen him on the TV show *Project Runway*, where he was one of the judges. In the fashion world, he's known as being a very professional and yet caring man. From the moment I walked into his showroom, I could tell he loved his work and absolutely put his heart into it.

Lindsey met me at the front desk and took me on a tour of the building. Every room we walked through oozed class. Every person I met bustled with energy. Lindsey showed me through the various design areas, the men's section, the marketing department, the PR department, and the mailroom, and then she escorted me back to the women's area where I was going to work. Throughout the building, people were sketching designs, meeting with clients, talking on the phone with media and advertising representatives, and planning photo shoots for magazines. Fashion Week—the citywide seasonal spectacle where all the designers showcase their upcoming lines—was coming up in February, and people were preparing a seating chart for the big show. That was no easy task, I was told, because everybody wanted to come to a Michael Kors show.

"We call this 'our home,'" Lindsey said with a slight smile. "Basically that's because we live here all the time. But we love what we do. We wouldn't want it any other way."

I got right to work. Hour after hour went by, and when it was time to leave, I couldn't believe the day had flown by so quickly.

The next morning when I came in, there was a completely new task for me to do. Each day was like that. Some days I'd be researching on a computer. Another day I'd design a marketing poster. Some days I worked with Michael Kors's mother. It sounds funny to say it. Here is this world-renowned designer in his midfifties, a talent-filled creative genius who could hire anybody he wants—and his mother works for him. She's a totally great lady—fun, with a cute and sassy personality. I loved every moment I spent with her.

I met Michael Kors in person only once. One afternoon when I was in the showroom, he came in with a few people around him. He's of average height, with blondish hair, and he's tanned but not bronzed. He dresses in his own clothes and always wears solid, neutral colors. That afternoon he was wearing a camel-colored pant, narrowed at the bottom, with a white shirt. He looked elegant and professional. There was an air of sophistication about him.

"Michael, meet Lauren Scruggs," Lindsey said. "She's one of our interns here, and she's doing a fabulous job."

Michael smiled and shook my hand. With that, he was off again and on to the next thing.

Working for Michael Kors had little to do with actually meeting the man. The experience was much more about immersing myself in that environment. During one week, my job was to dress three models for Market Week, which happens right before Fashion Week. During Market Week, buyers from stores like Saks, Barneys, and Macy's come in to a big conference room area in the designer's showroom. It sort of looks like a big closet lined with Michael Kors clothes for the next season. The buyers look over all the new offerings, so the pressure is really on.

The models and I had a lot of fun. For up to seven hours a day, we were stuffed in a tiny walk-in closet (roomy, but still a closet) where they got dressed. Basically all we did was play dress up all day long with fancy clothes—a dream come true for a girl like me. There were always snacks on hand—fruit, nuts, chocolate, and bottled water. People asked me if I was insecure around all those models, but I never felt that way. We just had fun together. All three of them were laid-back and down-to-earth. They told great stories and respected each other.

I realized how easy it can be to form stereotypes about people. I'd always heard negative stories about fashion models—that they were all stuck-up, or anorexic, or chain-smokers. But these girls were none of those things. They were wonderful people and worked hard. They were confident in their own way, but they didn't try to be something they weren't. They were just themselves.

Weeks ticked by, and the writers' strike continued. Most of my waking moments during each weekday were spent at the studio, but the weekends were free. Kristin, Lindsay O., and I vowed that we'd learn as much about the city as we could during those days off. Each Friday night we came up with a plan. Often we'd take the subway to a new section of the city and go exploring. We toured the Meatpacking

District and SoHo, Little Italy, Brooklyn, Staten Island, and Queens. We went to parks and restaurants and clothing stores and just walked along the streets with our eyes wide open. There was never a free table, so we just sat down with whoever was around and started talking. On Sundays we went to Apostles Church in the heart of the city. The services there were raw—not focused on entertainment, but focused on truth. Sometimes I'd just strap on my iPod and go running. I ran on the trails in Central Park along the Hudson River and often on the city streets. It felt like I was in my own little music video, running against a wall of people.

There's so much going on in New York that there's not a lot of time to sit and think. It's not exactly what I'd call a contemplative city. It's a city that pulses with culture and ambition and passion—and that's what we girls wanted to experience. We found that if people are in New York, they're almost always there with a specific reason in mind. They're dreaming of being artists or authors or dancers or designers or actors, and they'll sacrifice whatever it takes to reach their goals. It's incredibly expensive to live in New York, but we met plenty of young people who were doing whatever it took to get by. They'd work multiple jobs and almost never go out to eat or buy new clothes.

After I'd been in the city for two months, the girls and I went out to the Tick Tock Diner one Saturday morning. It's not the type of eatery you'd put in a NYC guidebook, but it was right down the street from our apartment, and we sometimes went there when we craved a big breakfast. I'd just downed a cheese and spinach omelet and was starting in on a short stack of pancakes when I noticed a text from Sami on my phone. "The writers' strike is finished. We're back on." I let out a little whoop.

On Monday I gave my notice to Lindsey and thanked her profusely for all she'd done to help me out. They threw a sweet little going-away party for me at Michael Kors with cupcakes and punch.

"Come back anytime," Lindsey said. "You belong in this city."

I had two days off between internships. It was just enough time to catch my breath. I'd loved my time at Michael Kors. It gave me an opportunity to see the inside view of an incredibly creative international industry. But I was looking forward to the next internship too. It was why I'd come to New York in the first place, and it definitely felt like the place I should be.

Next stop: *Gossip Girl*.

CHAPTER 12

Gossip Girl

Lauren

I peered up at the subway diagram and shaded my eyes from the early morning sunlight. In front of me, green, red, purple, yellow, and blue lines snaked and crisscrossed all over a map of the city. It was 7:15 a.m., my first day of work, and I needed to commute from this station close to my apartment in midtown out to Silvercup Studios in Queens. *Let's see, that means heading north to Central Park, then east under the river.*

At first glance, the routes looked like a big bowl of spaghetti. But the more I studied the map, I saw that my commute was fairly straight-forward. It would mean a thirty-minute ride, tops. *Navigating the New York subway is all part of the experience*, I reminded myself. I descended the concrete steps to the subway station, slid my MetroCard through the slot, and pushed my way past the turnstile.

Inside the packed subway car, people lurched and jostled each other as the train started off and picked up speed. The smell of fresh brewed coffee hung in the air. There was no Wi-Fi service in the subway, so no one could check their phones, which felt refreshing to me. This wasn't my first venture into the subway, but it was my first time during morning rush hour. Everybody looked similarly funky and cool, well-styled and hip; yet in spite of the similarities, I noticed how much the people on the train represented a human mosaic. All colors of skin sat side by side. I heard a cacophony of languages—Spanish, French, Italian, and Farsi, I think.

I straightened my shoulders with pride at the thought of stepping out into this new world. The people I'd met so far at Michael Kors had all been amazing. Most had been women in their late twenties and early thirties who were all eager to help others learn and grow and accomplish bold things. I hoped the people at *Gossip Girl* would be no different.

When we reached the borough of Queens, my subway station came up. I climbed off and walked a few blocks over to 42-22 Twenty-Second Street in Long Island City, the address of Silvercup's main lot. A little shiver went down my back as I reminded myself that this was the big time. Silvercup is New York's largest full-service film and television production studio. In addition to *Gossip Girl*, a bunch of other movies and shows are filmed there, including *30 Rock* with Tina Fey and Alec Baldwin.

My internship at *Gossip Girl* was set to last slightly more than two months. The studios sprawled out like a suburban mall. When I found the entrance leading to *Gossip Girl's* fashion department, I walked right in, blinking a few times as I took in everything around me. The doors had opened into a big room that looked like a huge closet. Racks of clothing stood everywhere. Two desks were shoved off to one side. I glanced down at the floor, old and wooden. The walls were still lined with torn-up magazine pages, but the pictures were all new since my quick tour last fall. Everything looked creatively put together, but nothing was luxurious or glamorous. It was a work center, plain and simple.

Sami met me with a warm smile and showed me around. To my left was a fitting room where the actors went when Eric dressed them. Another, smaller room was off to one side where alterations were done to make sure clothes fit each actor perfectly. Sami introduced me to everyone, and then I went to work.

One of my main jobs that day and over the next few weeks was returning clothes to various designers' studios throughout the city. Some of the outfits used on the show were purchased, but others were on loan from top designers. Eric Daman would connect with designers and pick out looks he liked, then bring in the various options for each character to try on. That way Eric could decide what worked best. After a scene had been filmed, someone needed to return all those clothes to the designers. That was me. Fortunately, I didn't have to drive. Mike, Eric's personal assistant, accompanied me as the van driver, and we headed out around the city.

I hadn't driven in the city at all, unless you count riding in the back of a taxi. I soon received my first lesson in how to park New York style. Simply put, there were never any places to park when we needed them. Ever. But we had to stop frequently. So Mike just pulled up next to the curb, or double-parked, while I ran inside and delivered the clothes. He often came along with me to help carry clothes into the showrooms, so over the next few weeks we racked up our share of parking tickets. When I stressed about that, he said with a grin, "Look, Lo, it's just the way you gotta do things in the Big Apple."

Some days I'd be on set to help with whatever tasks needed to be done while they were filming. *Gossip Girl* is this gritty, high-drama, prime-time soap opera for young adults based off the book series by the same name. It's set around a mysterious narrator who runs a scandalous gossip blog about the kids who live in Manhattan's Upper East Side.

The series starts by showing the "It" girl, Serena, coming back into town after an unexplained absence at boarding school and trying hard to fit in with all her classmates again. Blair is her best friend, but the two often fight, usually about guys. Chuck is the filthy-rich bad boy who schemes to make everybody's life miserable. Dan and Jenny are the wholesome brother and sister duo. And Nate is the golden boy who's trying to make his way in the world the best he knows how.

The whole series is sort of a racy, guilty-pleasure-styled TV show where all the characters are absolutely beautiful and everybody is extremely wealthy. They all wear the most fabulous-looking clothes, sort of like an East Coast version of *Beverly Hills 90210*.

Although the show portrays a world I would never want to inhabit, I saw my internship as an opportunity to be a "roaring lamb" in an industry that doesn't really understand people of faith. Before I'd left Dallas and told people I was going to New York, some would furrow their brows. "Are you sure you want to go to *New York*?!" they'd ask. "It's such a dark place." Because I believe God opened this door for me, I never hesitated to walk through it.

In fact, being on set is nothing like watching the show. Nobody is starstruck with each other, and everybody acts normal and simply does his or her job. There are probably twenty to thirty people working on the set at any time. After a while, you get to know everybody pretty well.

The lighting guys come on and get everything arranged perfectly. Stand-ins serve as doubles for the actors so they don't have to wait around while everything gets set up. Actors mill around rehearsing lines, drinking coffee, and joking with one another. Cameramen, producers, directors, and extras are all doing what they do. Each shot is repeated a bunch of times to get every scene perfect. Sometimes it will take hours to shoot a five-minute segment.

None of the scenes make much sense when you see them being filmed, because they're often shot out of order and you don't have the context of watching the overall show to figure out the plot. In one scene that I saw being filmed, Blair was in the living room of her house having a heated conversation with Serena. In another, Dan and Jenny were hanging out in their kitchen, joking around with their dad. As the scenes were being filmed, I was standing maybe thirty feet away. From that distance, it was hard to hear the specific lines of dialogue.

Eric Daman was wonderful to work with. Most days I'd work more closely with Sami, but Eric would often be there too. He had blond hair and a ready smile, and though he was constantly busy, he was always kind. He treated everybody—actor, production assistant, intern, it didn't matter—as professionals and with a lot of respect. I'd see him in the wardrobe department quite often and got to know him well.

XO

One day I was working with one of the guys on set—I don't remember his specific job—and out of the blue he said, "Lauren, what's up with you anyway? You seem different from other people around here, but I can't quite put my finger on why."

I shrugged. "Maybe it's that whole Dallas thing."

"Nope. Not that. What do you believe in, anyway?"

"Believe? You mean like . . . in Jesus?"

"Is that what it is with you?"

"Why?" I asked with a laugh. "What do you believe in?"

"Everything. Jesus. Buddha. Karma. Myself. I believe in truth . . . whatever that is."

Over the next few weeks we had a lot of conversations like that—not just me and that guy, but many of us on the set with one another. People might not have believed the same things, but it seemed like everybody was interested in talking about spiritual matters and getting to the heart of life. I never pushed my beliefs on anybody. I seldom started the conversations. They just happened. The people I met often acted surprised when they found out I was a Christian. I guess they expected me to make them feel guilty for something they'd done wrong. But when they found out that I was going to treat them with the same courtesy and kindness they'd been extending to me all along, they were genuine about things, and our conversations became deep and rich.

I read my Bible a lot, all the weeks I was in New York. I prayed all the time—not out loud during the day, but I'd write prayers in my journal, or pray them as thoughts to God as I rode in the subway back home each evening. For the first time in my life, I was completely away from my family. I wrestled with the idea of distinguishing my own faith from my family's faith. I'd never been alone enough to examine my beliefs like that before.

I thought about how I'd seen plenty of people back home whose faith seemed more like a hobby. Oh sure, they went to church and called themselves Christians, but that seemed to be the extent of it. I knew I needed my faith to be something more than that. It needed to be something real, something that encompassed every area of my life.

The book of Isaiah became my favorite. The entire book seemed so poetic, graceful, and rhythmic, if not always easy to understand. Again and again I came back to one passage, Isaiah 40:29-31.

He gives power to the faint,
   and to him who has no might he increases strength.
Even youths shall faint and be weary,
   and young men shall fall exhausted;
but they who wait for the LORD shall renew their strength;
   they shall mount up with wings like eagles;
they shall run and not be weary;
   they shall walk and not faint.

Seldom did I feel exhausted in New York—that wasn't what spoke to me from the passage. Even though the days at *Gossip Girl* were always long, I felt fueled by adrenaline, always on the go. But I liked the image in Isaiah of young people seeking and finding God's favor. I liked the promise that God gives power to renew people's strength. I pictured myself flying like an eagle, running forever and ever, walking on new heights. I felt more certain than ever that my faith was truly becoming my own. This was no passing fad in my life. Faith in God acted as bedrock, something I could base my life on forever.

New York was a great experience for me. I was busy soaking in the heights and depths of the city, dreaming about and planning my career. What I was doing in New York was exactly what I wanted to do for the rest of my life. Not to be working at *Gossip Girl* or Michael Kors specifically—but to be immersed in a world of creativity, art, beauty, passion, and greater purpose. I found I absolutely loved being in New York. I felt independent and confident and excited with all the possibilities in front of me.

In late spring 2008 I finished my internship at *Gossip Girl*, hugged all the new friends I'd made, packed up my New York apartment, and flew home. On the plane ride back to Texas, I created a picture in my head of the things I wanted to do in life. The image wasn't formed concretely yet, but the dots were there, waiting to be connected. They beckoned brightly, like the lights of Dallas Airport's runway just before we touched down.

As my parents drove me back to our home in Plano, I felt like I'd climbed to the top of Mount Everest. My season in New York City had been amazing. I'd seen so much, learned so much, and done so many new things. I felt bold and ambitious, ready to stay at that high level and continue higher still.

What I hadn't learned, however, was that along with great opportunity comes great temptation. A new path would soon uncoil itself and extend its offer to me. It would be a wide and broad road, and I knew very clearly it was a direction I should not take.

Even so, I would soon find myself longing to run down its destructive path.

CHAPTER 13

Strange Black Cloud

Lauren

During the summer after my internships in New York, I traveled a bit, celebrated my twentieth birthday, and interned for a short time at an inner-city ministry in downtown Dallas.

All that summer I stayed on my mountaintop. The internship at the shelter was wonderful. It was the same place where Brittany and I had volunteered in high school, and some of the same kids were still there, just older now. I tutored and served meals and played games with the kids. In a way the culture in the shelter was the polar opposite to what I'd experienced in New York, but in another way it was very similar. The similarity was mainly that working there made me feel independent and powerful. Like my life had a strong sense of purpose.

That fall I enrolled at Dallas Baptist University (DBU) to finish my bachelor's degree. I didn't want to return to Texas A&M, and by then I'd taken nearly every class I could at community college. My first choice was not to be in college at all, but I knew I needed a degree. The big plan with my schooling was to sprint to the finish as fast as I could and then return to New York, where I'd dive headlong into a career.

It made sense to go to DBU. Brittany had already been there for a year—she'd transferred straight from Texas A&M. The university was nearby in Dallas, about thirty minutes from our house. Brittany and I decided to live in the townhomes on campus. We didn't live together this time (we were only two doors away from each other), but it felt good to have my sister so close again.

I decided on a major—communications. I'd started a blog right after I'd come home from New York. Blogging helped me figure out more of my writing voice, and I began loving the writing process. My blog was titled simply *LoLo,* and right away it started to receive some good traffic. It quickly became a random collection of writings and pictures about the things I loved most—fashion, color, style, meeting new people, cooking healthy foods, and finding delicious places around town to eat.

I also started freelancing for a number of online fashion magazines. I'd met some good contacts in the industry, and one of the editors, Molly, took me under her wing and showed me the ropes. I started writing for *Fashion Reporters*, *SMU Style*, *MyItThings*, and *PR Couture*. Some of the articles were interviews with fashion industry insiders, and other articles were my reports from various shows and events. I loved the writing. When I wrote, I still felt connected to New York City, my second home. I felt like I was doing something purposeful, and I liked that a lot. Because, truthfully, I didn't want to be in Dallas just then. Nope. Not at all.

It wasn't that I didn't love my family and friends back home. Everyone was great. But returning to Plano after being in New York felt like coming back to earth after I'd been to the moon. DBU was an even smaller world within Dallas. Only about two thousand students lived on campus, so I started feeling like I saw the same faces every day—a definite change from New York culture. I felt like I was treading water. Not that I hated DBU. It was a good school, and in addition to our studies, we always found time for fun. We'd gather a bunch of girls and cook dinner and hang out. Or we'd meet up with a group of guys and play sand volleyball on the courts on campus. But after being in New York City, I had to admit that DBU felt cloistered to me. I had a hard time articulating it to myself. I liked the people I hung out with, but I wanted to be somewhere else. I wanted to be back in New York.

I wasn't dating anyone seriously, though I did enjoy spending time with Brandon, another student at DBU. Brandon was highly intellectual and philosophical. He would take an idea and toss it around, examining it from every possible angle until my head nearly exploded. He became a good friend—though never more than that. He asked me out a few times, but I was fairly sure I wasn't interested in anything romantic with him.

Brittany and I had a conversation about relationships one day toward the end of that school year. It was one of those rare moments after class when I was alone in my townhome, and Brittany came over. We curled up on the couch and kicked off our shoes. I poured us tall glasses of ice water with lemon wedges. Brittany was experiencing the normal ups and downs of the dating world, like we all were.

"Lo, how come when you like a guy, he doesn't like you back?" Brittany asked. "Or if a guy likes you, you can't stand him? Or if you both get along with each other, you don't have any romantic feelings for each other whatsoever?"

"I know exactly what you mean," I sighed. "I don't know why it can't just all work out for once."

I hadn't dated anyone seriously since Tim, a few years back now, and I was beginning to wonder if I would ever find that special someone. Brittany and I certainly didn't have any answers that afternoon.

XO

In the early part of the spring semester in 2009, the itch to be back in New York City was stronger than ever. An incredible opportunity came in early February when I got a call from an editor. Would I like to come to New York with her and cover Fashion Week?

Would I?!

Fashion Week is the term given to the prestigious, twice-yearly, international trade show where all the top buyers in the world preview the next seasons' line and buy merchandise for their stores. The main Fashion Weeks are held in four cities: Paris, London, Milan, and New York. Other shows are held in Montreal, Sydney, Seattle, Los Angeles, and several other cities worldwide. I'd always dreamed of going to New York's Fashion Week, but I never thought I'd get the chance to cover it as a reporter.

When I landed in New York, I went straight from the airport to the show. *Wow, oh wow.* People were taking pictures all over. Models were walking in and out. Huge names in the industry were everywhere. The whole experience was so intriguing to me. I felt overwhelmed with thankfulness to be there, and just buckled down, worked very hard, and wrote my articles. I absolutely loved every minute I was there.

That made coming back to Dallas Baptist even harder. As the semester progressed, I knew I definitely wanted to be back in New York again for a second summer. I prayed about it. I talked to my parents about it.

But—and here's where things got strange—the answer was always no. No. No. No. Not from my parents—they were okay with it.

But from *God.*

That's a funny thing to describe if you've never felt it before. I so strongly wanted to go back to New York and live there for another three months, but I had absolutely no peace about going there. Anytime I prayed about it—which was every day for several weeks—every answer was absolutely, definitively no.

And I couldn't make sense of that answer. Why would God say no to a good thing like New York—and say no so strongly within my spirit? There was nothing morally wrong about me going to New York. There was nothing specifically in the Bible that addressed the subject. It wasn't that I was like Jonah, the Old Testament prophet, who strongly felt God calling him to go one direction and then ran the other way to escape that call. I didn't know what else to do that summer other than go back to New York. I didn't feel pulled to Dallas necessarily either.

So I decided to go to New York anyway.

At first, everything lined up perfectly. Kristin, my roommate from my first stay in New York, would be coming to the city again too. We planned to share an apartment, although we'd be in a different part of the city, in an apartment owned by New York University. My immediate goal was to land a job. I didn't really care where. I'd worked retail in high school, and I figured I could find a similar job in New York. I wasn't seeking an internship this time. I just wanted to be in the city.

As the plane's wheels touched the tarmac at JFK International Airport, I couldn't help but remember one of the first Bible stories I'd ever learned as a kid: Adam and Eve in the Garden of Eden. When Eve looked at that fruit, she may have seen a perfect apple. Juicy and red. Pleasing to the eye and delicious to the taste. What would be better than taking a bite? But God—knowing something that Adam and Eve didn't—had told them no. New York was like that fruit to me. There was nothing wrong with this apple, at least nothing that I could put my finger on. But for whatever reason in his infinitely wise mind, God didn't want me eating this apple either.

I shook the thought out of my head, willfully walked off the plane, and caught a cab to my new apartment in the city.

CHAPTER 14

Forbidden Fruit

Lauren

Kristin was not coming to New York after all. Her plans for the summer had fallen through. That meant I was living in my apartment alone.

The day after arriving, I scoured the city looking for a job. I applied to store after store, but nobody was hiring. I couldn't figure it out. My résumé was strong. I wasn't looking for anything glamorous. I had plenty of retail experience. Finally one store said they had an opening for me, but they needed some paperwork from my insurance company. The store said they'd get it for me, and the wait wouldn't be long. But a day went by and then another. And then a week and then two weeks. Still no job. Time was running out, and nothing was working out as I'd hoped. I had no good reason to be in New York.

To compound the problem, the weather in New York was horrible for the first ten days or so. Just cold, cloudy, rainy. It was a disappointing start to what was supposed to be a summer of fun. I loved being outside, and it was harder to be out in crummy weather. I felt depressed. Lonely. Emotions I usually didn't struggle with—at least not for very long. It's a funny thing when you say no to God. At first God's voice is loud in your heart. Then it begins to get quieter, and you start to think he's okay with your rebellion. I stopped reading my Bible every day. I still wrote in my journal, but my entries became much less prayers and much more my worries about not having a job or not knowing what I wanted to do in life.

Eventually the sun came out. A family friend lived in the city. She was about the same age as me but already married. Her husband was in college, so she had a lot of days free. We went to Central Park together and lay out on blankets on the lawn. *Ah, this is more like it,* I thought.

Two weeks after arriving in New York, I got a call from an editor I knew. She'd heard I was in the city and asked if I'd cover a charity event set for that weekend. There might be more freelance work for me that summer, she added. I jumped at the chance. Finally things were starting to click.

Another reporter and I went to the charity event that weekend. We got our stories, then stayed to mingle with the guests. I spent much of the evening talking to this guy in his late twenties named Jordan, who asked for my phone number at the end of the night. I said okay, even though I don't think I'd ever given out my phone number to a guy I'd just met before.

Jordan was a member of the New York Yacht Club, and the next day he asked me out to an opening of the club's new river dock, so I went. It was a big party and really cool, and I felt almost like I was in Florida, seated outside on a terrace in the warm summer evening. I wore a short black dress, and I felt tanned and pretty as my hair hung loose around my shoulders. A lot of Jordan's friends were there, and I felt fairly safe. Jordan and I went out a few more times after that, and he kept calling me, but I didn't reciprocate much. He was funny and respectful of me, but I sensed our values weren't quite in sync.

A day or so after meeting Jordan, I went out with the other reporter to explore the city. We ended up in the Meatpacking District, which is one of the cool and trendy parts of town. A kid our age invited us to a pool party on top of the hotel where he was staying, so we went. The view up there was really impressive, and we looked out over a beautiful panorama of the city as the sun was setting. Since we didn't know anyone well, we decided to leave early. But before we could walk out, we met another guy, Mason, who I swear could instantly make any girl feel like the most beautiful woman in America.

Mason talked to us for some time, then invited us to a club down the street from the hotel. His job was in marketing. Specifically, he looked for attractive young girls and invited them to nightclubs at the owners' request. The theory, Mason explained, was that any nightclub with a bunch of pretty girls in it would attract more people and develop a more exclusive reputation.

Mason wasn't kidding. The first nightclub he took us to already had a huge line outside the door—at least an hour's wait. Mason escorted us straight to the front of the line. The bouncer smiled broadly, pulled back the velveteen rope, and whisked us inside without ever checking our IDs.

A table was already set up for us. Our drinks, we were told, would be free. I was only twenty and didn't normally drink, but I didn't want to insult Mason, so I sat sipping a vodka cranberry as the music pounded in my ears. Lights flashed all around us, and everybody I saw looked young and beautiful. I felt a wild daring rise inside me as I took it all in. Mason snapped his fingers, and a waiter brought me another drink. Ten minutes later a third drink mysteriously appeared. That was soon followed by a fourth. My body mass index isn't that high, but even with that many drinks in me I didn't feel completely out of control. Just foggy. The dance floor appeared hazy, and I felt a strange pull between wanting to dance like no one was watching and finding a quiet corner so I could lie down.

That's when the most gorgeous guy I'd ever seen walked up. He had tousled blond hair and deeply innocent gray-blue eyes, like a puppy that's just been brought home from the pound. The guy held my gaze for at least twenty seconds, then touched me lightly on the arm and leaned in close. "You are so beautiful," he said over the music. That was his exact opening line. *A bold move,* I thought, yet he completely pulled it off. His name was Brooks. He modeled for Abercrombie, and he was ditching this nightclub and heading to an even better one down the street. "Come with me," he said flatly. It wasn't a request.

"No, I can't," I said. The alcohol spun through my head. "I don't even know you."

"What does it matter?" Brooks said.

His smile was so incredible. His shoulders were so broad. What girl could ever be unsafe with him? I didn't know how to answer his question.

"Give me your number then," he said.

I nodded.

A few nights later Brooks called and asked me to go out with him and his friends. We went to the Meatpacking District again. He was wearing a stylish, short-sleeved rugby shirt, and I wore a chartreuse dress that was open at the shoulders. Brooks could get us inside anywhere, no questions asked about my age.

At the first club we danced and each had a few drinks. Then we went across the street to a restaurant, and he bought me dinner—sliders and fries with another couple of drinks. Then we hit another club and kept dancing. Every place we went was the utmost in chic. Sometime just after midnight he yelled in my ear over the blaring music, and I found out that he was originally from Fort Worth, which is only about thirty minutes from Dallas. We even knew some of the same people. *A hometown Texan boy*, I thought. *That seals the deal.* When the last club closed, it was four in the morning.

"Uh, I live kind of far from here," Brooks said.

"All right then." I took his hand with a smile.

We went back to my apartment. My mind was foggy from too many drinks. A little voice told me I was on slippery ground—and dangerous, too—to bring a guy I barely knew back to my apartment. But Brooks was so cute. So perfectly beautiful. Any girl would swoon over him. What was I supposed to do? Send the poor guy away in the cold?

Late the next morning I woke up, hopped in the shower, brushed my teeth, and got dressed. All I could think about was how much fun we'd had. Brooks had been a perfect gentleman. In the midst of kissing, he'd sort of given me that raised eyebrow like he was hoping for the next step in the game. But we didn't have sex that night. I was still a virgin, and I was committed to keeping things that way.

We went out for breakfast, and after that both of us had the whole day to ourselves. Brooks's modeling schedule was irregular at best, so he had a lot of free time on his hands. He went home to change, and then we met up again later that afternoon in Central Park.

Brooks and I spent every day together after that. There's a section in Central Park called Sheep Meadow. We'd meet around one in the afternoon, head to Sheep Meadow, and lie out in the summer sun. He wasn't a Christian, and whenever I imagined our futures together, logic told me that it would be very hard to have a deep relationship with a person who didn't strongly value the same things I did.

But I wasn't thinking very logically just then. I'd ignored the voice of God and gone to New York that summer. I'd been hanging around in questionable places where people were influencing me, not the other way around. And I'd fallen head over heels for a guy who I clearly shouldn't have been with, a guy who was expecting me to do things I didn't want to do. Deep down I knew it wouldn't be long until I succumbed to Brooks's expectation to go further.

On the one hand, I didn't want to have sex with him. It wasn't that I was a prude. To me, sexual purity isn't a rule to be followed—it's a gift from God. I see it as his way of freeing me from painful emotional entanglement now so that one day my husband and I can experience all the joy that sex was created to bring.

So I truly didn't want to go further with Brooks. But then again, I did. I truly did. I'd say my willpower had about two weeks left. Maybe one. Maybe it was only a matter of days. I felt a twinge of darkness somewhere deep within me, almost like a wave of nausea.

One afternoon a few days later, my editor called and asked if I could do one more freelance story for her. That made a grand total of two stories for the summer. Two whole stories. The sum total of my work in New York City, summer 2009.

Brooks and I kept seeing each other every day.

One morning shortly before my twenty-first birthday on July 18, I got up and looked in the mirror. If I had looked more closely at my reflection, I would have noticed that I didn't look normal. A weird yellow hue colored my skin. I felt tired, truly exhausted. If I'd been honest with myself, I would have admitted something was wrong, because I rarely felt exhausted. I took the right vitamins and generally ate clean. Another wave of nausea rolled around in my stomach, but I ignored it. That night Brittany was flying into the city with her boyfriend, and we were all set to celebrate our birthday together. Nothing was going to stop us.

This sounds weird to say . . . but it's an important detail when I think about it now. When I went to the bathroom that morning, my stool was strangely dark, like I'd eaten a full tub of black licorice the night before, and I hadn't had anything like that.

It might have been dread working its way through my body—that feeling of not being true to myself. Or it might have been some other sort of poison, something purely physical. If I had been listening to my body more closely, I might have been able to discern that I hadn't been feeling like myself—or acting like myself—the entire summer. Some part of my inner physicality was paying for the tension. I was going downhill, although I didn't know it just yet.

Truth was, I wasn't listening to myself. I wasn't listening to anyone at all.

I felt another wave of nausea but ignored it again. I threw on a fun tank top and a cute pair of jean shorts, grabbed my sunglasses, and headed out the door to meet Brooks.

CHAPTER 15

A Message I Needed to Hear

Lauren

"Your lips look all white, Lo," Brittany said. "Are you wearing sunscreen ChapStick or something?"

"Nope, not me." I picked up my purse and glanced into the mirror by my apartment's front door. "C'mon, hurry up. We'll be late."

It was Tuesday evening, four days before our twenty-first birthday. Brittany had just arrived in New York, and we were all set to celebrate together. Her boyfriend would fly in a couple of days later to join us, but tonight it was just the girls. We were meeting up with two girlfriends at a place near the Hudson for a special night out. I did feel woozy, like maybe I should lie down for a while. But I kept my mouth shut. There was no way I was going to spoil this night for Brittany and me.

The restaurant on the Hudson offered a fabulous view of the river. I ordered a chicken salad and picked at some breadsticks, but honestly I wasn't hungry. I went to the bathroom several times and kept thinking I was going to be sick, but nothing came up. I hadn't been drinking, so I knew that wasn't the culprit.

About 10:30 p.m. our friends left, and Brittany and I boarded the subway to head back to my apartment. The subway car was packed. I clutched the rail as the train lurched forward, and everything began to spin. I'd never fainted in my life, but I felt like I was going to pass out.

"You need to stand up!" Brittany had snapped into her motherly role and was speaking brusquely to someone occupying a subway seat. "My sister's not feeling well. She needs to sit."

I took the seat and put my head between my legs. "I'm okay, Brittany. I just need some air."

At the next stop we got out. We were at Times Square, a busy station, and I looked up at the flight of concrete stairs in front of me, wondering how I would ever be able to climb them. They led up out of the subway to fresh air. I took a shaky step toward them. Then another.

"Lo?" I heard a voice say. Maybe it was Brittany, but I wasn't sure. "Lo!" This time the voice sounded far away.

Everything grew dark.

When I woke up, I was on my back on the concrete, still underground. People's faces seemed to float above me. Feet walked straight past. Brittany knelt by my shoulders. She held her cell phone to her ear, calling an ambulance.

"I'm okay, Brittany, really," I said. "I just fainted." But she'd already flashed into action, becoming a warrior for me. My legs felt wobbly as I tried to stand. My stomach flip-flopped. How was I ever going to get to the street? Brittany would never be able to carry me that far. I sat down again and prayed one word: *Help.*

"Ma'am, you okay?" came a voice from above.

I looked up. A young couple, maybe in their early thirties, stood next to me. "Let me go get a bottle of water for you," the woman said. "There's got to be a machine around here somewhere." The man was talking with Brittany.

"Lo, he's going to carry you upstairs," Brittany said. I nodded.

This stranger—I so wish I had caught his name—carried me up two flights of stairs. The woman brought me water. "We're going to be praying for you," she said, which is something I hadn't heard before on the streets of New York. Then they were gone, vanished into the crowd.

A few minutes later the ambulance arrived. I kept telling the paramedics I was all right, but Brittany insisted they check me. They took me to an emergency room in a part of town I didn't recognize. The doctor on call figured I was either pregnant or drunk and gave me a urine test but not a blood test (which would have answered a ton of questions, we discovered later). He concluded I was dehydrated and told me to go home, get some rest, and drink plenty of fluids.

Dana Crawford was in New York just then, helping her son move into a new apartment, and she met us at the emergency room and filled out the paperwork for me. It felt good to have someone we knew so well close by. She made sure I was all right, and I really was feeling better by then—or at least that's what I told everyone. It all felt so silly. *Imagine me fainting like that.* Brittany and I took a cab home. I drank lots of water and ate some watermelon and went to bed.

For the next few days I basically just functioned. I wasn't feeling well a lot of that time, but our twenty-first birthday—something you wait your whole life for—was coming up. There was no way I could let this milestone pass by uncelebrated.

On the afternoon of our birthday, Brittany and I were out for lunch at a rooftop plaza, and I was feeling terrible again. I called my mom in Dallas about 1 p.m. She went online and found a travel doctor who was able to see me at 5 p.m. that same day. Brittany and I took the subway to his office. It felt hard to walk, and I kept looking for a place to sit down. The walls of the doctor's waiting room were painted a swirly green. A painting hung opposite from where we sat. Boats riding the waves. Ships with tall masts. Their sails flapped in the ocean wind. I blinked. The sails were actually flapping. Moving with each gust of the storm.

"Do you have an eating disorder?" the doctor asked inside his office.

"No, I love eating, and I hate throwing up." I remember my words exactly.

The doctor was kind and ran some tests but said there was nothing that could be done until the results came back. In the meantime he ordered me to take it easy. I agreed, at least in spirit.

I went home, took a shower, and lay in bed with my towel on. I felt too ill even to get dressed. I felt as though I might pass out but didn't say anything. Brittany brought me a basket of berries I had in my refrigerator. I ate the entire basket and felt a little better.

The wheels of celebration were already set in motion, and since I felt on the upswing, Brittany, her boyfriend, Brooks, and I went out that night. At four in the morning I found myself in Brooks's apartment with just the two of us in his room. We were lying on his bed, kissing, and my heart was racing.

"You are so-o-o-o-o beautiful," he whispered in my ear. His hands started wandering.

"Brooks." That was all I said. His name. I couldn't think of the right word then, the word I wanted to say. It was "no." But no other words would come out of my mouth.

"Wow, your heart is just pounding, Lauren. Are you nervous about this? Really, there's nothing to be afraid of. It's the best thing in the world. And you are so-o-o-o-o-o beautiful."

There were those same words. I'd heard them from him before. I thought I had already made myself clear on the subject. The answer was still no.

"It's okay," he added. "Really. You're so special to me."

"You're special to me too," I murmured, but I stopped kissing him.

"So what's wrong? Everything okay?"

I sat up. The walls in his bedroom were moving. "I don't feel very good, Brooks. Really. I just want to go to sleep now. Is that okay?"

Brooks nodded.

At ten the next morning I took a taxi home to my apartment. My stomach hurt. My head ached. Brittany and her boyfriend had gone to a museum and left a note. I climbed into bed and fell into an unsteady sleep.

An hour later the phone rang. The voice on the other end sounded strangely insistent. "You need to come in—right now!" It was the doctor's office. I called Brittany. She came back and got me, and we went to the doctor's office together.

"Lauren, this is serious stuff," the doctor said. "The results came back, and you're bleeding internally. Your red blood count is one-third of what it's supposed to be. You're suffering from malnutrition, and until we can figure out exactly why you're bleeding, we'll need to replace all this blood you've lost. That means a blood transfusion first thing tomorrow morning."

Bleeding internally?

That's why my energy levels had been so low. Why I had fainted. Why my heart had been racing. Why my stools had been so dark. My body was passing blood.

I called my parents and explained the situation. "I'll be there immediately," Mom said. She bought a ticket and within hours was on a plane to New York. My dad rented a hotel room for all of us. He called and told us to meet Mom at the hotel room. By now it was obvious something was wrong with me. Everything that was supposed to be red on me was either white or yellow. My lips, my cheeks—nothing looked normal. At the hotel I lay on the bed, and Brittany lay next to me. My body began to feel numb. It felt hard to lift my arms.

"Lo, you are so warm," Brittany said. "I can literally feel the heat coming off you." Brittany's boyfriend went out and bought a thermometer. My temperature was 104.

When Mom arrived, Brittany was on the phone with the doctor. My mom took one look at me and then took the phone from Brittany.

"My daughter can barely move," Mom said. "We need to get her to the ER immediately." The travel doctor told her to take me to Mount Sinai Hospital as quickly as possible.

By then I was out of breath and struggling to talk. I couldn't walk by myself. The bellman brought a wheelchair up to the room and took me down to a cab. It felt so good to have Mom there. Inside the cab, I lay against her. She carried me into the ER.

Hours ticked by. A regular hospital room wasn't available, so for much of that time I lay on a bed in a big ward with a curtain around me. The emergency room was absolutely jam-packed, loud and chaotic, and there wasn't much privacy. One poor woman nearby threw up every five minutes. Another person was screaming. Medical staff began to give me blood transfusions, one right after the other, four pints total. Night came, and I slept a bit, off and on, but there was no place for Mom to lie down. I could see that she was growing exhausted. She tried to doze in a chair, but that never works well. We tried to be patient. She prayed with me a lot.

We stayed in the emergency room at Mount Sinai for eighteen hours. Finally a regular hospital room opened up, so they moved me in there. Another patient was in the room along with me. Mom stayed on a chair in the corner of the room. Back at home, Dad was busy making phone calls, trying to figure out the next steps. The best plan was for me to go back to Dallas, to doctors and hospitals we were familiar with, but we were told that I wasn't able to fly until my hemoglobin levels came up.

Over the next couple of days the staff at Mount Sinai did every test they could think of—a colonoscopy, an endoscopy, a CT scan. Something may have gotten nicked in my upper intestine. No one was too sure. But one thing was certain: they needed to stop the bleeding— and quickly. People with a red blood cell count as low as mine don't live too long, they said.

I don't remember much from that time. Mostly I tried to sleep. I remember Mom murmuring to me once how pale I looked—absolutely colorless. I remember she braided my hair and put some blush and lipstick on me. It was so sweet of her, and the kind gesture made me smile. Still, no diagnosis came. I remember being so hungry. An IV pumped fluids into my arm, but because of all the tests they were running, I wasn't allowed to eat for the first two and a half days.

Finally on the fourth day in the hospital, my hemoglobin levels had risen enough so I could fly. Dad made reservations, and Mom and I boarded a plane for Dallas. That was the abrupt end of my summer in New York. Brittany had packed up my apartment a few days earlier. She'd brought all my stuff home with her.

Maybe it shows how out of whack my priorities were just then, but even though I was at death's door, my thoughts turned to Brooks. I found it weird that I hadn't heard from him since the early morning at his apartment. For the past month we'd been talking all the time, texting by the hour, hanging out with each other every day. Now there was nothing but silence.

I sent him a text. "I was bleeding internally, and they had to give me a blood transfusion." I expected sympathy, a caring word, at least a question about how I was doing. A guy who cared deeply for me would ask how I was doing and worry that I was going to be okay, wouldn't he?

"OMG," Brooks texted back.

One phrase. That was the sum total of his response. No follow-up call. No e-mail. No message on Facebook. Nothing. Maybe I hadn't explained myself clearly enough. Maybe there was something more I should have done.

I tried to give him the benefit of the doubt. But there was a word flitting through the back of my mind that I'd heard somewhere. High school maybe. The implications of the word were just dawning on me. I couldn't remember it exactly, because I'd never encountered it before, never seen it lived out in real life. It meant a guy who's only interested in one thing, and when he doesn't get that, he dumps you. There is no real friendship with this guy. No real caring or compassion.

Player.

That was the word. There was no way to sugarcoat the truth. Brooks had discarded me like yesterday's trash.

Back home in Dallas, the doctors at Baylor checked me out. They said I needed more tests, but thankfully I didn't have to be admitted again. For the next several weeks I went back and forth from home to the hospital. I had another CT scan, and I swallowed a PillCam—a miniature camera that checks your entire digestive tract. All the tests came back inconclusive.

But I wasn't okay. I knew I'd blown it in so many ways. My physical health was shot. My spiritual health was shot. I felt like the prophet Jonah being digested in the belly of the whale. I'd run away from God and been thrown over the side of a ship, only to be eaten by an unnamed monster. I couldn't even hope to be vomited out on dry land.

Desperately, I longed for someone to tell me I was going to be okay. That's all I wanted to hear—one short, specific phrase: *You're going to be okay, Lauren.* That was it, but nobody was telling me that. My doctors and family were all being truthful. I wasn't going to be okay—something was seriously wrong with me. It's not that I wanted anybody to lie to me. I just wanted to hear one credible word of encouragement. I didn't know how to ask for it. I didn't even know who to ask.

God, I prayed. *I know things haven't been the best between you and me lately. And I'm sorry about that. I truly am. Please—somehow—let me know I'm going to be okay.*

One afternoon while a test was being done, I sat and looked out the window. The summer sky, normally clear and blue, was overcast, hazy, and darkening. I deserved God's anger. I knew that. I'd blatantly thumbed my nose at him. I'd told God I knew better. I hadn't been true to myself or what I knew was right, and I'd said and done things I deeply regretted.

I had my laptop with me, and right then I felt a sudden urge to check Facebook.

I logged on, and there was a private message from Cindy Froese, a friend of my parents from church. Cindy and I knew each other only from a distance. I knew she was a solid woman of God, but I didn't know much more about her than that. Her message was short and to the point. No preamble or introduction.

"Lauren," she wrote. "I can't exactly tell you why, but just this moment the Lord has so strongly laid on my heart a specific message for you: *You're going to be okay.*"

It was the language of grace.

I shut my computer and wept.

CHAPTER 16

Reconciled

Lauren

They never did find out what was wrong with me.

My internal bleeding stopped as suddenly as it had started. My red blood cell count began to bounce back to normal. To this day, I've never experienced anything like that again, and whatever went wrong with me that summer in New York remains a mystery.

In the fall of 2009, I started back at Dallas Baptist University. It felt good to be back among a community of close friends who knew me and supported me. I began reading my Bible more and walking closer with God. I paid more attention to my physical needs too. I'd always eaten healthfully, but I renewed my commitment to eat clean. I began to experiment with various foods, paying attention to how they affected my body's energy levels. I cut out most sugar, gluten, and red meat, and ate almost solely fresh vegetables, fruits, and lean protein. Avocado made a good substitute for butter, Greek yogurt for sour cream, and stevia for sugar. My favorite foods became crunchy kale salads, grilled sweet potatoes, and blackened, lightly-oiled Brussels sprouts.

That September I flew to New York to cover Fashion Week again. This time I didn't sense the Lord telling me not to go to the city. I didn't see anybody there I shouldn't be seeing. I just attended the shows, then went to coffee shops by myself to write. I began thinking ahead to the next summer and lined up several interviews to explore more internships. The good people at *Teen Vogue* talked with me, as did the folks at *People StyleWatch* magazine. But nothing seemed quite right. By the time I flew home, I had no idea what to do except continue on with the next steps at school.

In mid-October I was at the gym one day when I received a text from Brooks. It was completely unexpected. I hadn't heard a word from him since the text he sent right after I got sick. Then he followed up with a phone call and explained how he had assumed I'd call him when I felt better. At first I sensed he was trying to pin his insensitivity back on me, but the more he kept talking, the more I fell under his spell again. I kept picturing all the fun moments we'd had together. When he called me again later that evening, his voice sounded so comforting. He was back in Texas for a while, he explained. Did I want to come over for dinner?

I knew I shouldn't. I knew he was nothing but bad news.

But I went.

Brooks cooked dinner for me. I was impressed. We drove over to Blockbuster and rented three movies to watch back at his place. I swear I had every intention of just watching the movies and talking, but ten minutes into the first movie we were making out. Again, his hands strayed to places they shouldn't have. Again, he was telling me how beautiful I was, how special, how much he'd missed me. Again, I was swallowing all that praise, hook, line, and sinker.

Once again, I had the good instincts to say no and stop before we went any further—but just barely. The next morning, I kicked myself. I kicked myself hard. What was I thinking?! This guy was not right for me. We weren't on the same track spiritually. He had not been there for me at all when I was sick. I was so stupid. Yet with one single phone call from him, I'd followed his lead like a dog on a leash.

I vowed I'd never hang out with him again. But keeping vows is not easy, I realized, particularly when those vows are born from willpower only. Brooks didn't call again, and I didn't call him. For most of that fall semester, I simply went through the motions at college. I buried myself in my studies, taking almost twice the normal academic load. But my mind was still on Brooks, even though I couldn't stand the thought of him. I couldn't understand why I was so attracted to this guy who was so wrong for me. Not only that, but I missed the inspiration of the city and being around people whose career aspirations matched my own. New York City is the land of achievement, and I so desperately craved a sense of accomplishment again. I felt depressed, stuck in my thoughts, and I didn't know how to move forward.

XO

One Sunday after church, Cindy Froese, the same woman who'd sent me that awesome Facebook message, met me in the lobby and asked how I was doing. I could tell she wanted an honest answer, and I don't know what exactly came over me, but I started to tell her everything. I'm not usually that way with people I don't know very well, but there was something so comforting about her presence, so trustworthy—I just spilled it all.

Cindy hugged me and cried with me. After we talked, she invited me to a program at our church called Steps, which had been developed from Celebrate Recovery, a program that first came from Saddleback Church. It sounded suspiciously like Alcoholics Anonymous, and I didn't have a problem with drinking. But Cindy explained that the program was for everyday people from all walks of life who want to overcome life's problems, no matter what those issues are. So I signed up. I figured it couldn't hurt. Brittany was in China then, working at an orphanage, and I didn't have any boyfriends on the horizon. That meant that, in spite of my heavy academic schedule, I had some free time on my hands.

I soon realized I didn't know as much as I thought I knew. The program was spread over sixteen weeks, and I quickly caught the vision. Our pastor, Matt Chandler, described the program as a way to address harmful tendencies and face them head-on with truth from God's Word.

The big goal is freedom. You want to figure out why you head a certain direction and then submit that to the Lord and move forward in wholeness. Each week we had homework. Then we got together in small groups and discussed what we'd discovered.

At first I figured the things we talked about didn't have much to do with me. Fears, resentments, worries, doubts. But the deeper we got into the program, the more I thought, *Yeah, actually this is me. I do stuff like this all the time.* For instance, while growing up in Sunday school, the Christian faith was presented to me pretty much as a list of dos and don'ts—at least that's how I perceived it. If I toed the line and kept the rules, I felt good about myself. But if I didn't, then I thought of myself as a bad Christian. The truth was I had been looking at the wrong benchmarks of what real faith is. I had never looked deep into my heart, where things really mattered. I was just looking at the outside.

I discovered I'd grown up a perfectionist. No matter what my age, I needed things to look a certain way, or I expected people to behave a certain way. I was attracted to outward beauty, behavioral refinement, external style, and good taste. Those things aren't wrong, but I realized that I'd allowed perfection to become an idol to me. The word *idol* was defined in the program as anything a person values more than God. For instance, I initially thought Brooks was the perfect guy for me. He was outwardly beautiful, and that's what I admired him for. I ignored God and chose Brooks instead. The perfect guy had become my idol.

When it came to guys in general, I saw another harmful pattern in myself. Part of me might have been honestly attracted to a guy, but another part of me might simply have wanted to get his attention. If I got it, then I felt good about myself. If I didn't, then I tried harder to attract him. An exchange like that didn't constitute a real relationship. It was only a game. I valued the approval of guys so I could feel good about myself, and I put a lot of pressure on myself to look or act a certain way and to always wear cute clothes.

Overall, I found out through the program that I was pretty horrible at expressing how I truly felt about things. I had learned a harmful habit of bottling my emotions deep within me. I stuffed them down and kept them under tight wraps where I felt certain they were safely stowed away. But every once in a while they'd leap to the surface. If something upset me, I'd never say outright, "This upsets me." I'd just let whatever bothered me silently simmer. Then a month later my emotions would explode. During my first stay in New York, I'd gotten into an argument with one of my roommates. It wasn't over anything huge, but I'd let my resentment build for so long that in the end, something small triggered my anger. After verbally lashing out at my roommate, I'd walked down to the corner in my pajamas to call my Mom and sort things out.

Cindy was my sponsor through the entire program. She never judged me. She walked me through each step with compassion, wisdom, and grace. She'd often say things like, "You know, it's really normal to feel that way." Or, "Actually, you're just fine. That's what most people do."

As one part of the process, I needed to write an inventory of my entire life under certain categories, such as fear, anger, and worry, recording everything I'd ever done in those categories. One afternoon I read my inventory to Cindy. We met for three hours, and the words poured out of me. It was such a peaceful experience to get all that weight off me. To just admit all my struggles and get them out in the open. Cindy is an amazing listener, and it felt good not to be trapped by any secrets. It was one of the most freeing moments I've ever experienced.

My life adopted a new sense of ease. The lure of Brooks faded from my mind. I felt forgiven. Free. For the first time I began to truly grasp what grace is all about. God loved me no matter what. I didn't need to perform for anyone, much less him. He was continually inviting me to good places, places that he had prepared for me, and I was overwhelmed by the strange mix of his power and gentleness.

That fall I took one more semester at DBU before graduating in December 2009, one semester early. I'd taken such full academic loads my last two semesters that I had more than enough credits to get my degree ahead of schedule. A lot of my friends were starting jobs, getting married, and moving on with their lives—but I had no idea what I wanted to do. Still, I felt at peace with that.

I decided not to return to New York in the summer of 2010. I spent that summer at home, working at a Mexican restaurant. It was a far cry from the glamour and glitz of New York. But it was a fun place to work, and I felt like I should just do something down-to-earth.

One day I went for a long drive, just thinking. I drove out of the city and saw the wide open spaces east of Dallas. The road seemed to stretch on forever in front of me. The road itself wasn't beckoning, but God's voice seemed to be calling me onward. *This difficult season is over*, he was saying. *And you came through it just fine. Now let's go on together, and you'll see what's around the next bend.*

Cindy had told me something like that once. "God wants to use you mightily for his purposes, in ways you can't yet imagine. But before he can do a work through you, he needs to do a work in you."

I smiled, turned my car around, and headed for home. I was eager to get on with whatever was going to come next.

CHAPTER 17

The Start of Something Wonderful

Lauren

Brittany got married.

She didn't marry that guy she had been dating when she visited me in New York, but this wonderful, happy bear-of-a-guy named Shaun Morgan. Shaun turned out to be everything her other boyfriend wasn't. The other boyfriend was an okay guy, but sort of dark, almost like he always wanted to separate Brittany from her family and clutch her all to himself. Shaun wasn't like that at all. He wanted to draw Brittany closer to her family, not further away. What was important to Brittany was also important to Shaun.

They'd met at Dallas Baptist more than a year before the wedding. In September 2009 they had their first date, and when Brittany came home, a couple of us girls hung out in her room, debriefing their evening. "This sounds weird to say so soon," Brittany confided. "But I have this feeling I'm going to marry him." We didn't think she was weird at all. We all knew Shaun, and we all knew Brittany. Both of them were easy to connect to, and we just knew it would work out between them.

Shaun and I clicked right from the start too, which was important to me. When you're a twin, you have extremely high standards for whoever dates your sister. But I was like, *This guy's great.* He proposed to Brittany during an unforgettable date on top of the headquarters of a bank in downtown Dallas. He'd arranged everything ahead of time with the security guard, who let them sneak in. Brittany was totally surprised—and totally happy. She said yes in an instant and never wavered in her decision.

For a few months during the middle of the engagement, I experienced moments of angst. I pictured Brittany and her husband living in their own little house, painting walls, arranging furniture, both heading out the door to work each morning. Some days I was completely happy for them. Other days I couldn't believe we'd actually grown old enough to get married. But the closer the big day came, the more I became genuinely excited for them.

The wedding itself was absolutely wonderful. Brittany looked gorgeous in a slim-fitting, floor-length white dress. I was the maid of honor. There were seven other bridesmaids plus a cute flower girl. We all wore purple strapless dresses and carried white bouquets. Matt Chandler, from The Village Church, performed the service. There was beautiful singing and a touching Scripture reading, and Shaun washed Brittany's feet in a symbolic act of devotion toward her. Everyone could see the love Brittany and Shaun had for each other.

Then we partied. Their reception was held in a lavish ballroom on the top floor of a building downtown. There were tiny white lights and gold-backed chairs and candelabras and flowers and a huge, frosty, four-tiered wedding cake. The band played really fun music, and everyone shimmied around on the hardwood dance floor. The whole event seemed like a divine evening. God was at the center of their wedding, and you got a sense that this is the way it's supposed to be.

Right around that time I made some of my own advances in the dating world.

There was this guy, James. He was that sincere, solid one I mentioned earlier, who girls lined up to date. Tall and broad-shouldered, James was the real deal. He wasn't a player at all.

One evening I was serving customers at Uncle Julio's Mexican restaurant, and James came in for dinner along with his older brothers. James was so cute. One of his older brothers was getting married in two weeks, and James didn't have a date to the wedding, so just on a whim he asked me out. I ended up not going to the wedding, but the ice was broken between us. We dated a few times after that, just casually.

James was a year and a half younger than me, which took the pressure off—no one urged us to get serious too quickly. We went out to dinner a few times, and I started seeing more of his substance and depth. He loved God and was committed to growing spiritually. He was working hard to pay his own way through college and planning to go to law school after he finished his undergraduate degree. On one of our earliest dates, we were driving back from dinner when a van flipped over on the freeway ahead of us and caught fire. James screeched our car to a stop, made sure I was okay, sprinted to the burning van, and helped pull the people out. Once the rescue crew had arrived and taken over, James hopped back in the car and sort of shrugged it all off, but I knew he'd done something genuinely heroic. That was just like James.

Neither one of us wanted to date exclusively at first, so we put any idea of a relationship on the back burner for a few months while we both focused on other things. But then in January 2011 we ran into each other again, and it was like no time had passed between us. We went rock climbing together at a nearby indoor facility, then went out to dinner a few times and just had a lot of fun. The weeks passed, and as we started spending more time together, I knew this was becoming serious. We started calling each other boyfriend and girlfriend, and I realized that's what we now officially were. I felt safe with James. Secure. I genuinely liked him. When I secretly considered our future together, I circled around the picture cautiously, but I knew that if I was with a guy who had the same qualities as James, we would have a really good shot at something wonderful together.

I knew it for certain one night a few weeks into 2011 when James came over to my house for dinner. My parents were out of town, so James and I went out and got some food, came back and ate it, then watched a fun movie together on the couch. At about midnight we kissed each other good night; then I opened the front door so he could leave. Ten inches of snow had unexpectedly fallen in the past hour. What were the odds of that? It never snows in Dallas!

James called his mom, and she told him absolutely not to drive home (nobody drives in the snow in Texas). We both nervously laughed about the predicament that put us in. How convenient. But James slept on the couch, and I slept in my bed. It just felt good not to have a boyfriend pressure me physically in a situation when he could have. Having James sleep over felt . . . comfortable, I guess. Like we were at home together, and relaxed with each other, and we could be like that for a long time to come.

About that time I started a new hobby: boxing. I've always stayed in shape, but I wanted to try a different workout regime, so I found a great coach, Rudy Barrientes, a former national Golden Gloves Champion. I bought some fun pink boxing gloves, went to work, and absolutely loved it. Rudy showed me the fundamentals of the moves, and we started sparring every other week. The hits were full force from me, and maybe half force from him, but he wasn't exactly hitting me softly. I loved the challenge of the sport. The physicality. A person can't be hiding in a shell when she's in the center of a boxing ring.

The world of style and fashion still mesmerized me, and I looked for ways to stay involved with that industry. I quit my job at the Mexican restaurant and started working at a clothing store to help pay bills. In March 2011 I flew to France to cover Paris Fashion Week. I'd never been to France before, although I'd covered the Montreal Fashion Week a few months earlier and been exposed to French-speaking culture a bit.

A good friend of mine lived in Paris, and she offered to let me stay with her. She worked long days, so her boyfriend, Mathieu, a Frenchman, offered to take me on a tour of Paris shortly after I'd arrived. Mathieu had a little moped, and I sat behind him as he drove me past all the famous sights—the Eiffel Tower, the canals and bridges along the Seine River, and the majestic flying buttresses of the Notre Dame Cathedral. Paris is an absolutely breathtaking city.

Early the next morning I needed to find my own way to the venue where Fashion Week was being held. I'd studied some French language guides before the trip but didn't speak much more than a few words, so I immediately got lost in the Paris subway system. The people of Paris were much more gracious and helpful than in the tales I'd heard about Parisians, and I soon found my way to Fashion Week and connected with some photographer friends I knew from New York. They were having an equally confusing time navigating the city, so for the rest of the week we hung out as a team and got lost together.

The designers and industry insiders at Paris Fashion Week were surprisingly more relaxed than the people I'd encountered in New York. Maybe it's the European sophistication thing, but everybody in Paris was down-to-earth and far more welcoming than I'd imagined. I loved meeting the models—they were so free, their styles were amazing, and their personalities were great fun.

The editors I was writing for wanted the articles to absolutely drip with description, so one of my pieces for *Fashion Windows* began with this illustrative opening, which I hoped met their expectations of liquidity, while offering a touch of humor.

Ann Demeulemeester [a designer] lavished undeniable beauty upon us at her show on Wednesday as models were transformed into hybrid birdlike creatures. Saturated in pure black, this collection focused on dramatic leather details, Amazon warrior reflections, and belts loaded with feathers as armor. Spiked hair dyed black and white echoed Cruella De Vil in the most sartorially pleasing of ways, and when it should have been intimidating, it was just simply a manifestation of beauty and strength.[4]

When Fashion Week was over, I flew back to America, hugged James hello at the Dallas airport, and went back to my parents' house. Life felt good, like things were really beginning to click on a lot of levels. I had a great boyfriend. I had a part-time job to pay the bills. I had strong connections with the fashion world and was becoming an established freelance writer in it. There was only one thing missing: an actual career.

But I had some big ideas for that.

For the past several months I'd been planning, dreaming, hoping, praying, researching. I knew what my perfect job would look like, but I also knew nobody would hand it to me on a silver platter. I was perfectly willing to work for someone else and figured that's what I probably should do first, to learn the ropes. But one of my editor friends had turned the tables on that idea awhile back when she suggested I should just go out and do it myself. This woman was in her late forties and had really been giving me a leg up in the industry.

"It's really hard to find your perfect job," she said. "Why not create it yourself?"

Create my own job, I thought. *Y'know . . . I think I could do that.*

CHAPTER 18

LOLO Magazine

Lauren

I dreamed of a magazine that would inspire people to live their lives out loud.

It wouldn't be just any ordinary young women's magazine. It would capture the true vitality of life—purpose, drive, color, beauty, and fun. I wanted to create a magazine that would showcase all the paradoxes of young women's personalities—something serious yet lighthearted, something important yet also whimsical. I didn't want articles to read like stodgy academic journals or hard-hitting news reports. I wanted them to sound like cool conversations, like the ones I had with other girls in our dorm rooms at college, or the ones I had with other young professionals at busy New York street corner cafés.

Already, I knew on a personal level the taste of true enthusiasm, when a person has great excitement for a subject or a cause. I loved art. I loved travel. I loved fashion. I loved beauty. When a person is truly enthusiastic, she's free to live in light of what God has called her to be passionate about. That's what I wanted this magazine to hold out to other young women—an invitation to be truly enthusiastic.

On the beauty front, I wanted people to see how character is the highest aesthetic a young woman can have, and how character is expressed not only in how a woman looks but—particularly—in how a woman acts. On the fashion front, I wanted people to be able to take the high-street editorial images they saw in magazines and translate those looks into their own style. On the food front, I wanted people to know how to eat healthfully and experience optimum energy for everyday living. On the travel side, I wanted people to be culturally well-rounded and experience worlds beyond the bubble of their hometowns.

That's what my magazine would be about: food, fashion, beauty, health, and travel. But the twist would be practicality.

Anyone could live out loud.

That's the message I wanted my magazine to convey.

Molly, one of the editors I'd worked with, had offered me a lot of advice career-wise. She encouraged me not to wait for the right opportunity to come along but to make it happen myself. I prayed through the idea, talked to my parents, and knew this was the direction I wanted to go. Molly helped me formulate a business plan and set me in motion, then set me free.

I soon enlisted the help of a good friend, Shannon Yoachum. She was in her last semester at the University of Texas and headed for a career as a fashion journalist. I invited Shannon to Fashion Week in New York City, where we spent a lot of time talking through the magazine's conception. Although she has a strong personality, we soon found that we worked well together. We understood each other's ideas, and our working relationship felt natural and complementary.

We began working together on story ideas and on how we wanted the magazine to flow and feel. We created a logo, wrote sample articles, and secured illustrations. But just when things were really coming together, we hit a snag. Our web builder fell through, and we didn't have a lot of money left by then. We knew that a high-quality, custom site like we wanted would cost at least ten thousand dollars to create. Through a referral we met Josh, a talented young designer, who created our site perfectly, then sent us the bill. "I believe in what you're doing," he said. His bill was—miraculously—less than a thousand dollars.

After months of preparatory work, launch day finally arrived in August 2011. We had all our content ready. Everything was laid out and positioned in different sections. In previous weeks, we'd sent out announcements on social media sites. Finally, we counted down from ten, took a deep breath, and turned on the website. *LOLO Magazine* had officially come to life. We formally announced the magazine's beginning on our Facebook and Twitter feeds and crossed our fingers. We were expecting a few hundred hits the first day. At the end of the day, we checked our stats. Our magazine had been viewed by more than four thousand visitors. It was a huge start!

Every day was a learning process. We set a goal of researching and writing three new articles per day. Though we soon found out that was an overly ambitious pace to maintain, we kept working hard. We met with people in the industry, went to fashion events, and interviewed insiders. We experimented with subject matter and found out which articles connected most strongly with readers and which ones turned out to be duds. We secured pictures and wrote captions and learned how to best position articles and features. Other companies began to contact us with products they wanted us to review or events they wanted us to cover. We managed the social media that drove the exposure—posting our articles on sites and answering comments. We handled the business aspect of things, learned about advertising and marketing, and took care of taxes.

Despite all the work we were putting in, we were hardly making any money—far less than minimum wage. But we expected that. Our goal for the first year was to grow our readership, and after that to secure a strong advertising base. After launch day, our numbers dipped into the hundreds, but then quickly and steadily rose.

The magazine was always on my mind. It felt like a newborn baby. I worried over it, prayed over it, and stayed up at night feeding it. But mostly, I just enjoyed it. I truly loved every second of what I was doing.

Running *LOLO Magazine* was my dream job. The possibilities of where it could go seemed endless. Each day's pace was brisk, but we soon learned to delegate more and contracted with freelancers to write some of the articles. We enlisted the help of a couple of college interns. One of our correspondents lived in New York and was positioned to get the inside scoop on what was happening there. Both Shannon and I stayed active in every part of the magazine's functioning. We quickly branched out into video, and I did interviews with actor and model Kellan Lutz from the hugely popular *Twilight Saga* movies, fashion designer Rebecca Taylor, and my former colleagues from *Gossip Girl,* actor Chace Crawford and costume designer Eric Daman.

What I loved most was how people said the magazine was truly connecting with them. People felt inspired by what we did. Because of our articles, they experimented with style. They traveled to other cities. More than one person told us they changed college majors as a result of our magazine's influence. We didn't talk directly about God much in the articles, but more about "life at a deeper level." We weren't afraid to incorporate faith into all aspects of life. I felt like a roaring lamb.

XO

With the magazine launched and running smoothly, I focused again on personal matters. In November 2011 James and I decided to cool our relationship. We'd been on-again, off-again in recent months, but it felt like now was the time to call it quits officially, at least for a while. It wasn't that I didn't love him. I did. Very much.

But—hoo, there were complications.

The closer we became, the more I realized just how serious this relationship was becoming. At our age, we weren't dating simply to date anymore. We weren't fourteen and hanging out at the movies. We were in our twenties, and our dating had become intentional. We were considering spending the rest of our lives together, and we both took the prospect of marriage extremely seriously. When we decided who to marry, we both wanted it to be the firmest decision we'd ever make. Neither of us wanted to have any doubts in our minds.

But in my mind, doubts kept poking up.

Not about James, actually. Overall, he was great. Sweet, kind, loyal, fun. But about myself.

When I looked honestly into my heart, I knew I still considered other guys. I didn't know if that was normal—if everybody felt that way when they were in a serious relationship. Was I the only one in the dating world who wanted to keep her options open as long as she could? Maybe the problem was that I simply couldn't commit to the great guy I was with.

I prayed about it all the time. I talked to Brittany and Shaun about it. I talked to my mom and dad about it. I talked to some other wise women I knew. They all saw the complexity of the situation. I was getting mixed signals about what I should do. Everyone loved James. Yet they understood that I needed to be clear on things if we were to proceed, and I wasn't clear. Some thought I should go another direction. They were confident that someone else was out there for me—I just hadn't met him yet.

One wise woman even had a highly specific dream about me and some imaginary guy. He and I were married, far into the future, with three beautiful young sons named Hudson, Dawson, and Canyon. Those names didn't come from me. I'd never mentioned anything like that to her, and I had no idea what to think of all that. I couldn't discern if her dream was a fluke, the result of a slice of bad pizza she may have eaten before bed, or if this woman was truly seeing into the future—like perhaps the homeless man had done years ago.

His predictions had come true for both Brittany and me. Just as he had said would happen, my world now contained innovation and travel and writing and celebrities. I hobnobbed with VIPs and was aligned with "eminent people of the world," just as he'd foreseen. (Although . . . I had to say there was one more thing the homeless man had mentioned—something about me fighting battles—that hadn't come true yet. I wondered about that every once in a while. But I figured maybe it referred to starting my magazine.)

None of us could see into the future. That's why making a decision about James was so difficult. He was an amazing young man—concrete and solid and real. I so desperately didn't want to lose him. But in my head I vacillated back and forth between being sure and being unsure, and so I needed to be honest with him. James needed his future wife to hold him as number one in her life. But until I could figure this out, or until God clearly showed me the direction to go, I didn't want to lead James on. He deserved all of me—and I couldn't give that to him yet—so I had to let this play out. I had to see if God was steering me in another direction. And that's why I broke up with James.

"Promise me you'll be really careful, Lo," James said when he dropped me off at my house the night we broke up. "I can't quite explain it, but I have this feeling like something bad is coming your way."

I nodded, and we hugged, even as I shivered a little. James was always there for me. He sees God's purpose in things, even difficult things. What more could a girl ever want?

On Wednesday night, November 30, 2011, I wrote what would become my final journal entry for some time. I set my pen down, turned out the light, and pulled the covers up around my chin. Tomorrow was Thursday, a new day at *LOLO Magazine*. I felt good about that, like I always did. And then there was only one more day after that until the weekend. I was looking forward to Saturday. December 3. Brittany and Shaun were coming over to decorate the Christmas tree early. I knew we'd have a lot of fun. After that we were planning on going to church in the evening, and then over to our friends' house for dinner.

I hoped Dad could make it. He'd been looking worn down lately.

I sure hoped he wasn't coming down with a cold.

CHAPTER 19

A Painful Journey Back

Jeff

The wind blew from the north on the evening of December 3, 2011. And when the steady gusts of Oklahoma air pushed south along the Highway 75 corridor and reached the Aero Country Airport in McKinney, Texas, the wind's direction set into motion a series of events that would change our lives forever.

I wouldn't learn this simple fact about wind direction until months later when I visited the accident site for the first time. I had been in constant contact with Mike (the owner of the airplane) since the accident. But I had yet to visit the crash site for myself. Nothing within me wanted to go there. The thought of seeing the place where my daughter nearly died brought the horror of that night back up again. And those were memories we were all desperately trying to put behind us.

Still, I needed to learn as much about the accident as I could. The Federal Aviation Administration (FAA), the courts, and the insurance companies were wading through the countless legal issues surrounding the accident. Meanwhile, there had been a lot of baseless speculation from others about what had happened that night. I had learned early that it was better to stop reading the online comments below the myriad of news stories that came out after the accident. The majority of comments were positive and encouraging. People expressed their sympathies and wished Lauren a speedy recovery. But a small segment of comments were accusatory, mocking, and even cruel, which is a typical result whenever people develop opinions based on speculation or jump to conclusions. The most hurtful comments were from people who called Lauren a "dumb blonde" and assumed she must have been drunk, high on drugs, or texting. Regardless of stance, everyone seemed to have an opinion about the accident—both the people who supported Lauren and those who ridiculed her. I didn't want to answer all these people's questions, nor would I be able to. I just wanted to see the accident site for myself.

On the afternoon I toured the airport, Mike personally showed me around. The sky was overcast and had a glare that made me squint. Seeing the site proved too emotional for me at first, and for a while I just walked around the tarmac silently, choking back tears. I wouldn't learn everything I needed to know about the accident that day, but Mike was able to clarify some things for me.

In northwest Texas, Mike explained, private airport runways are typically built from north to south, because generally the wind originates from only those directions, and wind direction dictates which way a pilot will take off, land, and park the plane.

That's precisely what happened the night of December 3. With a north wind blowing, the pilot landed the plane and maneuvered it off the runway onto the taxiway, as he should have. He parked the plane on the tarmac behind Mike's hangar. The plane's nose faced north, because a pilot is trained to park a plane facing into the wind.

The plane's design offered only one point of entry and exit. The door was located on the right side of the plane. This meant the plane's door faced east toward the taxiway, not west toward the hangar and the house. If the wind had been coming from the south, the plane's nose would have faced the other direction, and Lauren could have climbed

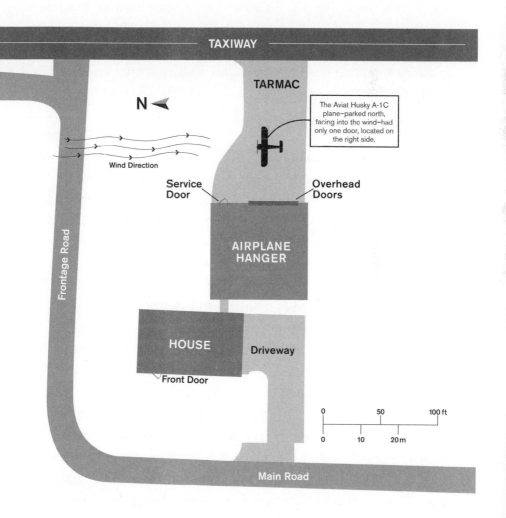

RUNWAY

TAXIWAY

TARMAC

N

The Aviat Husky A-1C plane—parked north, facing into the wind—had only one door, located on the right side.

Wind Direction

Service Door

Overhead Doors

AIRPLANE HANGER

HOUSE

Driveway

Front Door

Frontage Road

Main Road

0   50   100 ft

0   10   20 m

out of the plane and walked in a straight line directly into the hanger and the house. But because the plane was parked to the north, it meant that when Lauren exited the plane she needed to walk in a semicircle around the plane to return to the hangar and the house. When she climbed out of the plane, I suppose she could have turned to the right and walked around the back of the plane. But instead she turned to the left and walked into the propeller.

There was a logical reason she did this.

Newscasters widely reported two potentially misleading terms: that Lauren was a "fashion model" and that she had flown in a "private plane." I understand how Lauren could be mistaken for a model, but she's never done any modeling except for Dallas-area friends and their photography businesses. She's never considered herself a model or called herself one. One news report even called her a "supermodel," which made Lauren shake her head with a mystified smile when she heard about it later. ("Supermodel" is a highly specialized term that applies to only a few of the world's top models, such as Kate Moss and Gisele Bündchen.) The private plane part was partially correct, but the problem is that when people hear those two terms in proximity—"fashion model" and "private plane"—it's easy to envision some sort of glamorous celebrity walking down the steps of a sleek corporate jet.

That wasn't the way it happened.

The plane Lauren rode in was a 2011 Aviat Husky A-1C. It's a tiny, utterly basic bush plane. If you're a hunter in the Yukon or a mail carrier in the remotest sections of Alaska, this is your dream airplane. Its mission is to take off and land on dirt roads, fields, and mountainsides. The plane features two seats total, one behind the other, and a tight-fitting empty space in the back where you could squeeze in a dead elk along with a sleeping bag or camping stove. Stem to stern, the entire plane is only several feet longer than a Ford Taurus. The cabin height is just four feet, and the cabin width is just twenty-seven inches.[5] Picture a flying canoe. An enclosed kayak with wings and a motor.

This was the second Aviat that Mike had owned, so he was familiar with the plane. The pilot who flew that night had clocked tons of time in Huskys and tail-wheeled airplanes. The plane's operations were nothing new to him.

The narrow cabin area became one factor in the accident. You don't stand up and walk around inside the cabin of an Aviat Husky A-1C. You don't gracefully walk off the plane or even climb down a folding staircase onto the tarmac like you do from a small commuter plane. Climbing in and out of the Aviat Husky A-1C is no easy matter, and there is no placard on the inside or outside of the plane that explains the techniques. To get in, there is a stirrup on the lower part of the plane's exterior that's intended to be a footstep. Then there is a grab bar near the top of the plane. If you put your foot in the stirrup and grab the bar up high, you can swing your legs up and get in the plane. To climb out, you basically reverse the order. Mike explained that it feels like climbing backward down a one-step ladder. Mike noted with a chuckle that when his oldest son took the test for his private pilot's license, the FAA examiner got stuck in the plane for a full twenty minutes. This is one tight plane.

Compounding matters further, the door of an Aviat Husky A-1C looks nothing like an actual full-framed commercial airplane door. It's more like a car window that's hinged in the middle. One section (the glass part) opens upward, while the other section (a metal part) opens downward—like two halves of a clamshell. This means that the stirrup I mentioned above is largely blocked from view when exiting the plane.

Then, slightly off-center of the door, two long stabilizing rods (called wing struts) attach to the bottom of the plane and extend upward from the base of the plane to the farthest tip of the wing. To climb in or out of the plane, a person needs to navigate around the struts.

Located in front of the struts are the plane's front tires. The tires look like you should be able to climb on them to use as a step when exiting the plane. The easiest way out pushes you toward the front of the plane rather than the rear.

When Lauren climbed out of the plane, it's safe to assume she exited in the manner that would feel most natural to her—presumably by going forward onto the tire. Picture Bo and Luke Duke from the old TV show *The Dukes of Hazzard* sliding out the window of the *General Lee*. A few days earlier Lauren had been flying in a different plane that had larger, balloon tires, and when she flew in that plane, she had probably learned this other method of exiting a plane—by stepping onto the tire. So that way of exiting likely felt most natural to her.

There is footage of the accident scene, which was taken by the fixed security camera mounted on the rear of the hangar. The tape proves some things, but even then all the details aren't conclusive. Mike has seen the video, along with FAA administrators, but I haven't. According to Mike, due to the way the plane's body is positioned between the camera and the plane's door, it's impossible to see Lauren exit the aircraft or impact the propeller.

Nevertheless, exiting the plane by stepping in front of the wing strut would have put Lauren in harm's way, because it would have placed her on the side of the strut closest to the propeller, not closest to the tail of the plane.

So why didn't Lauren see the propeller?

Next time you ride in a commuter plane, the kind that takes you from a hub city to a smaller airport, take a good look out the window at the propeller. Even at moderate airspeeds, a spinning propeller disappears. You can look straight at it and see landscape on the other side like you'd see through a picture window. The propeller itself becomes a faint, smudgy circle—almost invisible. Some propellers are partially colored red, which creates an effect similar to placing a reflector in the spokes of a bicycle wheel, and in perfect weather conditions during daylight hours, you can see a faint red circle. But Lauren's accident happened on a drizzly, dark evening, with no stars out and a limited moon. There were strobe lights on the plane and a taxiing light on, as well as light coming from the back of the hangar, but Lauren climbed out of the plane on its darker side. The propeller would have been impossible to see at night.

Which brought up the last question in my mind: Could this have happened to anybody? This required some research at a later date than the afternoon of Mike's tour.

The technical term for being hit by a propeller is "prop strike," a broad term that refers to any time an airplane's propeller contacts anything other than air. This contact might be with flying birds, treetops, the ground, the top of a mountain, animals on the ground, or humans. In 2011 the FAA reported more than ten thousand wildlife strikes, many involving plane propellers, and acknowledged that the number is undoubtedly higher.[6]

A more precise description is a "prop-to-person" strike, the term given by the FAA to reference only propeller to human contact.[7] Prop-to-person records began in 1982 and include accidents involving both helicopters and airplanes. A friend of mine reviewed the records from 1990 through Lauren's accident on December 3, 2011, and eliminated the helicopter accidents, leaving only airplane results. The numbers showed that during this twenty-one year time period, ninety-one serious or fatal prop-to-person accidents with planes occurred.[8] Serious injuries included fractured arms and legs, severed fingers and limbs, and being struck in the head. Each year, an average of four people in America experience the same type of accident Lauren did. In other words, even though a prop-to-person strike is not as common an accident as, say, a highway collision, over the past two decades there is ample evidence of people walking into still-spinning airplane propellers.

The records showed that the people involved in these accidents worked in a variety of careers, including civil engineers and medical doctors—obviously highly intelligent people. One of the more widely-publicized prop-to-person strikes happened in 1983. Jack Newton, one of Australia's most successful golfers in the 1970s and 1980s, had a near-fatal accident when he walked into a spinning propeller of a Cessna airplane he was about to board at the Sydney Airport.[9] It was dark at the time, and there was heavy rainfall, which greatly reduced visibility. The accident cost him his right arm and eye, and he also suffered severe abdominal injuries.

Newton was at the height of his professional career at the time. You might expect that life was pretty much over for him after the accident. But fortunately he came back in big ways. It wasn't overnight, though. Newton spent months in rehabilitation and needed multiple surgeries, including facial reconstruction. Eventually he returned as a television and radio golf commentator and a newspaper reporter. He went on to design golf courses and travel as a public speaker, as well as serving as the chairman of the Jack Newton Junior Golf Foundation. Newton even taught himself to play golf again—one-handed. From his right-handed stance, he learned to swing the club with his left hand. Today, he scores in the mid-80s.

Jack Newton made an amazing recovery. But in the tense weeks following the day of Lauren's accident, we didn't know if life for our family would ever return to normal again. I say this because there was one more factor in the accident we learned about, a fact that became one of the most difficult for us to get our minds around. We learned about this from the surgery reports, and it relates to the propeller itself.

Immediately after the accident, Mike covered up the propeller with gunnysacks and tape to prevent the news media from taking pictures of it. For days to come, reporters and TV crews milled around his house, hoping for a lucky break. They were all over his property, in his driveway, in his backyard. Mike even caught people trying to break into the hangar. He had turned the propeller over to the FAA, per regulations. It's currently sitting in an FAA evidence room in an undisclosed location and set to remain there for the next two years. The plane itself was taken in the dark to a shop in Kansas to be repaired. The prop that was on the plane originally, the one that hit Lauren, had two blades. The prop on the plane now has three. There's no real advantage in a three-bladed or two-bladed prop, Mike explained; it's just whatever the pilot prefers.

Yet the blade remained a key factor due to two of its characteristics: speed and shape. The Husky's engine idles at about 625 to 675 rpm.[10] This means that at idle speed each blade of the propeller moves in a complete circle no fewer than ten times every second. An airplane propeller is not flat like a butter knife. It's curved like a windmill in order to grab the air. What we found out was that only the edge of that swinging windmill caught Lauren, but because it was curved, the edge caused a huge amount of damage. How much of the propeller touched Lauren? Picture the width of one and a half dimes.

One sixteenth of an inch. That was the sum total of the propeller's blade that touched her. All that damage to my daughter was caused by the merest hint of moving steel.

To me, that's one of the darkest, most ironic parts of this accident. If only Lauren had been positioned the slightest fraction of an inch in another direction, the blade would have missed her entirely. On the other hand, if the blade had struck one-sixteenth of an inch closer to her subclavian artery, she almost certainly would not have survived. Such a random, miniscule partition separated life from tragedy that night. So many random factors swirled together into a perfect, horrific storm.

Knowing that the accident could have happened to anybody doesn't make it any easier in my soul. I so wished I could have been there that night. I don't know for certain whether there is anything I might have done to prevent the accident. Maybe kept my eye on my little girl more closely.

After seeing where it happened, I kept examining the details of the accident, over and over again. I couldn't help it. Maybe that's what a father's heart does when there are so many things he doesn't know.

What I do know for certain is that the wind blew from the north that evening, and all would have been different, if only the wind had blown from the south.

CHAPTER 20

The Next Twenty-Four Hours

Brittany

The paramedics who treated Lauren later told reporters that when they first arrived at the accident scene, the extent of Lauren's injuries "took their breath away."[11] With the large amount of blood she'd lost, the lacerations to her head, and her skull fracture, the first responders thought for sure she wouldn't survive. Or if she did, there would be significant brain damage.

During that first long night in the hospital after the accident, our family was gradually introduced to the severity of Lauren's injuries. We'd heard the magic word "stabilized" earlier that same evening, so we were fairly certain Lauren wasn't going to die. But the other question—whether or not she would still be the same Lauren—loomed large in our minds.

The medical staff was sensitive in their approach to filling us in, yet they were honest, too, and we didn't want them to be any other way. Everyone we met that night who cared for Lauren was truly amazing. It helped to soften the wave after wave of bad news that came our way.

The brain surgery came first, I remember. The surgeons had to remove bone from her skull that had broken and lodged in her brain. This was one of the most frightening parts of the night. There is a great deal of difficulty in such procedures, the surgeon explained, and much could go wrong. The left frontal lobe of the brain, where Lauren was hit, controls a person's personality, including impulse control, social behavior, memory, and language.[12] Many people with brain injuries never completely recover, and for the rest of their lives they display irrational, aggressive, or inappropriate behavior. Even if Lauren's brain did function normally again, she would probably need to relearn all basic functions, beginning again as a little child would.

As the hours wore on, the litany of harsh news continued. I just felt stunned that night. I think we all did.

When the brain surgery was completed and was determined to be successful (as far as they could tell that night), another team of surgeons worked on Lauren's hand. It had actually been severed just above the fleshy part of the base of her palm. If it had been severed an inch higher on the arm (at the wrist), they might have been able to reattach her hand. But as it was, the hand was destroyed, and they needed to amputate the remaining tissue even farther, taking everything off just below her wrist bone. That way she'd be able to wear a prosthetic easier, they explained.

Lauren's left collarbone had been completely shattered. There wasn't much of it left, and another team worked on her shoulder and upper chest to stabilize the area.

Her eye had been sliced almost completely in two, and her skull and facial bones had been fractured both above and below her eye socket where the blade had hit. Surgeons installed plates under the skin above and below her eye to provide rigidity to the area. They planned to remove the eye the next day, after her body had rested awhile, but at 6 a.m. they changed their plan. The one bit of bright news was that they'd seen some cells in the eye starting to repair themselves, so they were going to try and knit the eye back together, in hopes that she might see out of it again someday.

One of the continual problems throughout the night, said surgeon after surgeon, was the need to clean out Lauren's wounds and prevent infection. The propeller was as sanitary as any piece of exposed steel, I guess, but it had noticeable traces of grease, dirt, and bug remains on it, like you'd expect to find on the grill of a car. They had cleaned the wounds as thoroughly as possible, but they were honest in reminding us that Lauren was still highly vulnerable to infection.

At about 7:30 a.m. on Sunday, December 4, the hospital's staff told us to go home and get some rest. Surgeons planned to begin their attempt to repair Lauren's eye at 10 a.m., and they expected her to be in surgery until 4:30 p.m. There wasn't anything we could do in the meantime, they explained. We didn't want to leave, but we saw the wisdom in it. Everyone had been up all night and in a constant state of tension. My dad was dealing with a bad cold on top of everything else. He was particularly wrecked.

Shaun and I went back to our house and tried to sleep for a while. Then we got up and drove over to Mom and Dad's house. I don't think anyone had slept more than fifteen minutes. Mom said they had just tossed and turned. Dad spent most of the time pacing around the living room, a cell phone in his hands. He had a nervous, panicky look in his eyes, even when we got there, and Mom told us Dad had kept saying, "We need some people here with us. We need people around us." I feared that Dad himself would need to be hospitalized soon. He was in total shock, alternating between acting panicked and behaving like a walking zombie.

Soon our good family friends, David and Elizabeth, arrived. Then Chris and Dana came over. Mike and Shannon. Chris Wilson. Brian and Tammy. Other people trickled in the rest of the day. By noon, sixty people filled the house. People brought casseroles, vegetable trays, and baskets of fruit and bread. It felt like a reception after a funeral. Dad spent most of the afternoon on the couch sandwiched between David and Brian. Dad lay in the fetal position, utterly exhausted, his head on David's lap.

Friends began to take charge of our family's functioning for us. Lo's best friend, Caroline Clark, set up a communication website on

CaringBridge.org, along with my mom's friend Sharon Kendall, the mom of Carter, the guy Lauren had sort of dated in ninth grade. The purpose of the website was to get updates out to family members and friends and to communicate specific prayer requests to people. Sharon and Cindy Kitchen volunteered to organize all meals. Another couple, Tracy and Denise Metten, stepped forward and rented a hotel room for my parents near the hospital, so they could spend every waking minute with Lauren and wouldn't need to drive back and forth to the house in Dallas through traffic every day.

People everywhere were following the story. Calls and e-mails started coming in almost immediately from people wanting to donate money for the inevitably huge medical bills. Sharon said she'd set up a bank account to receive donations.

XO

Throughout the day while Lauren was in eye surgery, my parents were in contact with the surgical intensive care unit (SICU). About every thirty minutes another phone call came with a new update on Lauren's condition.

Later that afternoon, just before Lauren got out of surgery, we went back to the hospital. About one hundred people were already there, standing outside the SICU, waiting for us. James was there. Shaun had texted him earlier to fill him in, and Shaun and I both gave him a big hug. "Whatever it takes," James said. "Whatever she needs."

"I know," Shaun said and gave him another big hug.

I'd say we were all sort of functioning again by then. Even Dad. When Lauren came out of surgery, they let the immediate family go in to see her. Lauren wasn't technically in a coma, but she was completely unresponsive—in a heavy, induced sleep due to all the medication she was on. When we walked into the SICU and saw Lauren lying there, Dad lost it again. He couldn't stop crying. Lauren had a breathing tube down her throat and a feeding tube in her nose, and she was hooked up to a wall of monitors. Mom was more pragmatic, I'd say. She was mentally rolling up her sleeves, bracing herself for the marathon of care to come. We were allowed to stay only a short while.

The story was first aired on the TV news in Dallas that evening. Just a local station reporting. We didn't even see it until somebody told us about it. A local kid gets into an accident. We didn't imagine anything would come of the story.

Anything at all.

The medical team explained that Lauren would be heavily drugged all Sunday night—the second night after the accident—with no possibility of waking. So they sent us home again. Mom and Dad went to the hotel near the hospital, and Shaun and I prepared to go back to our house. We knew the head of the SICU, a nurse named Carol, from church. She said she'd look in on Lauren throughout the night. We felt more secure knowing Carol was there.

Shaun and I walked to the parking lot outside the hospital, got into our car, and sat silently for a moment. He put his hand on mine and held it tightly. I looked straight ahead out the windshield, then made the mistake of turning and looking into my husband's eyes. While Lauren was in surgery all that first night, I had kept it together. Mostly, anyway. The next day when I had seen my parents so shaken at their house, I had kept it together then, too. Today when I had seen Lauren in the hospital bed, I purposely hadn't allowed myself to cry. Half of Lauren's hair was shaved, her head swollen to the size of a beach ball. I had no idea if my sister would ever be the same person she'd always been. Yet through it all I had steeled myself.

No matter what happened to my twin, I'd do whatever was possible to help her get better. With every ounce of strength I had, I would be there for her. The decision had been made instantly, even long ago. I knew all our family had made the same determination, Shaun included. I could see it in his eyes. We were just processing it in different ways.

Right then I decided I would never cry except in one place. I would cry only while sitting in our car outside the hospital next to my husband. He was my new safe place, and we were in this together.

I buried my head on Shaun's shoulder and fell apart.

CHAPTER 21

Flickers of Recognition

Cheryl

That second night after the accident, after Lauren had come out of her extended eye surgery, Jeff and I left the hospital at about 8 p.m. and drove a mile over to the hotel room that our friends had reserved for us. We couldn't even talk to each other. Normal communication was impossible. All we could do was breathe. I don't remember what we ate, or even if we did eat dinner. I remember taking a shower, getting into pajamas, and lying on the bed. Jeff had his Bible open to Psalm 46. Over his shoulder, I read,

> God is our refuge and strength,
>   a very present help in trouble.
> Therefore we will not fear though the earth gives way.

Our earth had just given way, and I knew God was our refuge and strength. But I was so weary. So completely wrung out. Deep down I knew that God had known this accident was going to happen—that he could have stopped it, but didn't. So God must have a purpose for this. The answers weren't going to be worked out immediately, but that bedrock thought in the back of my mind—that God was sovereign and had a good plan for Lauren—kept me going.

Jeff and I turned off the lights and lay in the dark. I wanted to sleep, to forget everything, but slumber was far off. I wanted to pray, to say something to God, to hear something from God, but I couldn't get my mind around any specific words. Maybe there was a praise song I could sing in my mind, part of a devotional I could recall, a verse to linger on that I'd memorized once. But I couldn't even remember what I'd just read over Jeff's shoulder. Exhausted, I watched the clock blink 12 midnight, then 12:30, then 12:45. I so longed for sleep.

Just before 1 a.m., one word came to me. I said it in my mind as a prayer.

Jesus.

He became the reservoir of all my hopes, the receiver of all my angst, the foundation of all my securities. Everything I couldn't process or articulate was caught and encapsulated in him. I knew Jesus could sort out all the prayers I couldn't even begin to verbalize. I began to pray that one word over and over again. *Jesus . . . Jesus . . . Jesus.*

When I looked at the clock again, it was 5 a.m. I'd slept. I was sure of it. Jeff had too. Four hours of sleep was better than nothing. They'd told us we could see Lauren again at 6 a.m., so we were at the hospital again precisely at 6:00. "Has she moved?" I asked the on-call nurse. "Has she opened her eyes? Has she said anything?"

The nurse smiled politely. She shook her head no.

Out-of-town relatives began to arrive. My two sisters flew in, as did Jeff's sister. Again that morning the waiting room became packed with friends. Either Jeff, Brittany, or I stayed in the room with Lauren all through the morning while others went out to talk with people.

As I sat in my daughter's hospital room, I watched how her eyes remained closed. She lay motionless in bed. I kept thinking of what the surgeons had all told us, how this was going to be a long haul and not to expect any signs of progress for days, weeks, perhaps even months to come. I kept praying, praying, praying—we just needed some sign of life. A tiny movement. A word even. Something. Anything.

Midmorning on Monday Lauren went in for another surgery so doctors could complete more work on her hand area. This time the surgeons wanted to close up the wound, which was a good thing because the wound had been left open since the first hand surgery. A closed wound meant less risk of infection. Meanwhile, I struggled. I knew God was there, but my human flesh was devastated, wishing I could take Lauren's place. Already I felt emotionally exhausted and helpless. How I longed to be able to snap my fingers and end what felt like a terrible dream.

Sometime later that morning Lauren came out of surgery. Back in the SICU room, Jeff was holding Lauren's hand. He was looking intently into her face and stroking her forearm. "Lauren," he said softly. "Lauren," a bit more loudly. "Lauren—if you can hear me, squeeze my hand." I don't know why Jeff said this. Maybe it was impulse. Maybe he was putting into words what we'd all been praying.

Instantly Jeff started crying.

I had seen it too. Unmistakable. A flicker. A tiny spark of movement. Our girl was fighting. Lauren had moved her hand.

Jeff asked Lauren to do it again, but one squeeze was all there was in that moment. One tiny squeeze. It didn't matter. A voice from the outside world had pushed its way through the mass of clouds that surrounded Lauren's mind. She'd processed the signal and responded. *Amen*, I prayed silently. *Jesus, thank you.*

Later that afternoon, after the tube from Lauren's throat had been removed, the speech pathologist came in and asked us if Lauren had spoken yet. We shook our heads no. "Go ahead and ask her to say something directly," the pathologist said. "See if she'll respond."

Jeff took the lead, pulling Lauren's hand into his. "Lauren, it's Dad. We're all here with you. If you can hear me, say hi."

Jesus, I prayed. *You can do all things.*

This time it was quicker. Some brief moment of recognition passed across Lauren's face. Her good eye opened halfway, then closed. The corner of her lip moved. Another flicker. Another spark. We held our breath.

"Lauren, if you can hear me," Jeff repeated, "say hi."

"Hi," Lauren said, in the merest whisper.

There was nothing more after that. No recognition. No hand squeezes or words. About an hour later, my sister sat beside Lauren. "It's Aunt Sue," I said. "Lauren, say hi to Aunt Sue."

The room was silent, then . . .

"I love you," Lauren murmured.

Her first full sentence. We were on top of the world!

That's my Lauren! I thought. *She'll fight hard and fast to get better.*

Almost simultaneously, though, I had to fight a flicker of disappointment when Lauren said nothing more. That was just one of countless times I experienced conflicting feelings. On the one hand, I was grateful to God for his mercies and proud of my daughter's determination and strength; on the other, I still found it hard to believe that Lauren was in SICU, and I worried about her reaction when she became aware of just how much she'd lost.

Medical staff explained that Lauren might be hearing and understanding things, even though she wasn't able to speak much. In times like these, patients can get confused because they know they've been in an accident but can't verbalize the question to ask what happened. That afternoon Brittany sat on Lauren's bed and spoke softly to her. She explained to Lauren that she had been in an accident and had sustained multiple injuries. As Brittany spoke, Lauren squeezed her hand. We all saw it. A little later on, Brittany asked Lauren if she knew her own name.

"Lauren," she said.

Such small victories. We cherished every one.

Hospital staff said people outside the immediate family could come into the SICU room, and a few people came in to talk and pray with us. College friends of Lauren's. People Lauren had worked with. Neighborhood friends. Lauren stayed mostly unresponsive. James came in at one point. Jeff said James's name loudly and asked if Lauren remembered him, but there was nothing. James didn't take it personally.

XO

Sometime later that day, Sharon Kendall motioned me out in the hall, a calm yet concerned look on her face.

"I needed to take my phone number off the CaringBridge site," she said.

I nodded.

"I'd put my name on there in case people from the church wanted to help," Sharon added, "but the calls haven't stopped. ABC, NBC, newspapers, tabloids, television shows. They're even calling from Europe."

I let out a sharp breath. "I'm not sure what to do either," I said. "They've been calling my cell phone all day too, and I've been letting them all go to voice mail." My cell phone number had been on the website for our ministry. I'd assumed the media had found the number there. Same as Sharon's, my calls were from regional, national, and international news sources.

A friend of a friend, Janee Harrell, was media savvy and volunteered to field the calls. A short while later, Janee told us that both *Good Morning America* and the *Today Show* had contacted her. They wanted us to make statements on national TV. The interviews wouldn't be taped—we'd be live. I talked to Jeff about it. The accident seemed like a private, family issue. We both felt numb. What was there to say? At first we concluded that we wouldn't do the interviews. But in the spirit of seeking wisdom from trusted friends, Jeff called our pastor, as well as another friend who's a national speaker, to understand other viewpoints. "It's actually in your best interest to make a comment," the friend explained, "because the media will tell this story regardless of your participation. If you agree to talk with the media, then it usually goes better for you, because you'll get a chance to tell your story the way you want to." Our pastor concurred.

So we changed our minds and agreed to the interviews.

A press conference was set up for 5 a.m. Tuesday morning. We did the interviews one right after another. We had no notes with us and no extended length of time to collect our thoughts. That's probably how they wanted us to appear—exactly like we were—raw. Jeff and I prayed before we went on, then answered the questions the best we knew how.

Ann Curry, from the *Today Show*, was very gracious with us. She asked if we thought it was a miracle Lauren was still alive.

"We're so grateful to the Lord for saving her," Jeff said. "Lauren has a strong faith in Jesus Christ, as we do as a family. We've been surrounded by friends who've been praying. It's been a horrendous few days, but we do see some bright signs ahead. She's a strong girl, she's physically fit, she exercises and eats healthy. Lauren's going to fight."

Ann asked about Lauren's character, about how she'd need personal toughness to survive. This time I answered.

"Lauren's always been a go-getter," I said. "She will use it for good, and she knows that Jesus uses everything for her good. She's going to have a tough time when she finds everything that's happened. Losing her left hand is really a tough thing, but she'll fight. She's a fighter."[13]

Right after that, George Stephanopoulos interviewed us for *Good Morning America*. He was equally gracious and asked us about the prognosis so far. We told him about Lauren speaking for the first time.

George asked if we were able to piece together any better what had happened on the tarmac. We didn't have any news other than what had already been reported.

George asked me what I had personally seen at the accident site, which is when I broke down and said, "I was just able to hold her. That's the toughest part of it all, just seeing her [lie] there and waiting for help."[14]

When the interviews were over, Jeff and I went back to Lauren's room. After the great strides she'd made the day before, we hoped for more strong progress today. We prayed specifically that Lauren would say some more words. More than that, we longed to see some genuine movement in Lo's body, even before the close of that day. We pressed God for more healing for Lauren.

Matt Chandler's wife, who is also named Lauren, is a beautiful and godly woman, and she visited us later that day. She's a gifted musician and asked if she could sing over Lo. Music has been known to trigger mental activity, doctors said, as well as to calm and reassure a patient, not to mention the family. She sang Lo's favorite worship song, "You Are Faithful." A flicker of recognition crossed Lo's face.

Michael Bleecker, our church's worship pastor, came into the room later and also asked if he could sing. Michael had been a tremendous minister to all of us in the waiting room the first night of the accident, and he had played songs then, too. He began to sing the song "Restoration," another favorite of Lauren's that we sometimes sing at church. The song draws inspiration from Psalm 30:11, "You have turned my mourning into joyful dancing" (NLT).

Jesus, I prayed silently, *please let Lauren's body move. Something. Anything.*

Michael kept singing.

Jesus, you can restore all things, I prayed silently.

And, slowly, as Michael sang the last chorus of "Restoration" . . . very slightly, Lauren lifted up her foot.

CHAPTER 22

The End of Week One

Jeff

The news hit with a fury. By Tuesday, December 6, we had dozens of requests from media sources. Huge names. *Anderson Cooper 360°*. *20/20*. *Entertainment Tonight*. TV shows and newspapers around the world. People wanted updates on Lauren's condition, but they were also asking us to do longer interviews and special features.

We drove back to our house on Tuesday to get some clothes, and a regional camera crew was on our front lawn. Two reporters from other stations hovered at our front door. We were caught unaware and told them, politely, that we weren't giving interviews just then. Inside the house, our answering machine was filled with more messages. About half were from well-wishers, the other half from news sources. A friend of ours passed along the name of a public relations company he'd worked with, A. Larry Ross Communications. Founder Larry Ross had experience handling high-profile cases, like ours was now becoming. He brought his senior team over to our home the next morning, and we felt relieved to turn the whole media side of things over to them.

I couldn't understand why the story was drawing so much interest nationally, not to mention from around the world. Sure, Lauren had started her own magazine and interviewed celebrities. But her magazine was just getting underway, and she wasn't exactly well-known herself. It was true that she was a remarkable girl—I'd known that since the day she was born—but lots of fathers think that about their daughters.

Someone said that the sheer contrast of the story had captured people's attention. Here was a girl, beautiful enough to be pictured alongside the fashion models she wrote about, who'd been in this horrific accident. And now she was fighting to come back—and fighting hard. People rooted for a girl like that. She had spunk and drive, and people could put themselves in similar positions and imagine how it would feel if something cherished were taken from them. *If that were our family, what would we do?* people wondered. *How would we find the strength to go on?* People found the story inspiring. On the CaringBridge website, people wrote that they were not only praying for Lauren, but they were drawing strength from her determination.

We quickly learned, though, that while widespread exposure can sometimes be your friend, sometimes it's not. Because of the media coverage, more people were praying for us and cheering on Lauren in her recovery, and we felt good about that. But the administrators at Parkland Hospital needed to install extra security guards for Lauren's sake. People were calling the hospital, eager for any bit of news that hadn't been reported. Strangers came by. Some offered condolences and brought presents. But others—well, we weren't sure exactly why they were there. For safety reasons, hospital staff changed Lauren's name on all charts, directories, and listings to a code name: Sky. That was the only name some nurses ever used for Lauren. "Hi, Sky," they'd say when they came into the room. "How're you feeling today?"

By late Tuesday morning, Lauren was moving around more in bed and had said one or two more words and sentences. She'd been accurately responding to voice commands from therapists most of the morning, wiggling her toes, and even raising her arm and her legs. She had taken a nap, and we all thought she was still asleep. Brittany came in the room, and Lauren opened her eye and said jauntily, "Hey, Britt." Later she told a nurse very clearly, "Thank you," and then she said to all of us, "Sorry I've been sleeping so much," which made us laugh.

Tony and Candice visited Lauren that day. Candice is Chris and Dana Crawford's daughter and was about five months pregnant at the time. Lauren had known about the pregnancy before the accident. When Candice came into the room, Lauren was asleep. Lauren opened her eye, looked directly at Candice, and held out her hand. "Can I see your baby bump?" Lauren's voice was as clear as day. Candice smiled, and we all laughed. She moved closer to Lauren and let Lauren run her hand along her stomach. It was a beautiful moment for a lot of reasons. It was also a sign that Lauren was remembering.

But despite all the positive steps, I confessed that I wasn't doing well deep down. Any adrenaline I'd felt at the start had long since worn off. My cold seemed to be better, but I hadn't slept much in days. I felt exhausted and frightened. A man wants to charge ahead, to slay a dragon, to be active in the process of caring for the people he loves deeply. But I felt as if I couldn't do anything to help. Fear twisted around my gut like a python around its prey. There were so many moments of each day when all I could do was sit and wait.

Undoubtedly, my biggest worry was the trauma to Lauren's brain. Although she was talking a bit already, the bigger question of whether she'd return to being the same person we'd always known her to be loomed heavy in my mind. The doctors couldn't predict what the outcome would be, though at one point Lauren's neurosurgeon told us something that helped us put her progress in perspective. He said that if one hundred neurosurgeons had been gathered in a room and asked to review Lauren's initial charts and images, at least fifty of them would have predicted that she would never again form a complete sentence and would experience a personality change. At that moment, I realized how miraculous her progress had been, although undoubtedly the road ahead was long and uncertain.

In addition, all the practical questions a father asks himself had begun to jab at me. Of course I'd wondered, *What if Lauren never fully recovers?* But now I was doing some mental math of the most pragmatic kind. My question was simply: *Healing or no healing, how are we ever going to pay for all this?*

We were very willing to do whatever it took to help our daughter, but being in ministry didn't give us much financial leeway. Cheryl and I no longer worked in the corporate world. We'd retrained as marriage counselors, and we earned some money from our counseling service. We also brought in a little income from speaking at seminars and churches, and we got a very tiny bit more from the sales of our book. Due to the accident, our main means of generating income had stopped until we could get a handle on what Lauren's new situation would look like.

Then there were Lauren's medical bills. Even after insurance I knew the bills would be huge. I started adding it all up: Paramedics. A helicopter. Teams of surgeons. Anesthesiologists. Intensive care. Therapists. A hospital stay with no end in sight. And even if Lauren recovered, what expenses were going to come next? Ongoing therapy? More surgeries? Prosthetics? Even changes to our house? All the unknowns put a huge strain on me. I envisioned bankruptcy for Lauren or a lifetime devoted to paying off her bills.

Our good friends Steve and Mary Farrar had visited regularly since the accident. Steve is a tall, barrel-chested, California-transplanted-Texan who writes books and speaks around the country at men's retreats and seminars. He's a few years older than I am and had been a real support during the last few days. On Wednesday morning, the fourth day after the accident, Steve called me early in the day, asked how I was doing, and told me not to lie.

"Not very good," I said. "Honestly, I don't know how we're going to make it over the long haul."

Steve didn't say anything at first. I could hear him opening his Bible, flipping through the pages. Then he read part of Isaiah 30:15 out loud. "In quietness and trust is your strength" (NIV).

"Jeff, this is where you're at right now," Steve said. "Your world's chaotic, but all you can do is follow the example set forth in God's Word. Wait calmly, remain quiet, and maintain confidence that the Lord is at work in Lauren's life—and in your and Cheryl's lives, too." Steve sat in solidarity with me for a few moments without saying anything. If he'd been with me in person, he would have given me a hug. We talked some more, and then we prayed together over the phone.

XO

Steve's words from Scripture became our rallying cry. Whenever I started looking beyond one day ahead, I got overwhelmed. But I consciously told myself that because God is in control, I could be calm. I decided not to try to see the future, only the next small stretch of time. Our new motto became "Twelve hours at a time."

That was good because on Tuesday night we needed to place a no-visitor policy around Lauren. No one except immediate family was allowed to see her. The risk of infection was still too high, and she needed optimum quiet and rest. Doctors were particularly concerned about her facial nerve healing correctly. Lauren's face had been slashed from the top of her head down to just above her mouth. If the facial nerve didn't heal, Lauren wouldn't be able to smile the same way or lift both eyebrows. We prayed specifically for the nerve to heal.

On Wednesday morning—Lauren had still spoken only a few words—hospital staff wanted to see if Lauren could sit up, and even more, if she could walk. Her vital signs were all good, and they wanted to get her up and moving around as quickly as possible. There's no sense for a person to lie in bed when she could be moving, they explained. Muscles atrophy if a patient doesn't move, and then recovery takes that much longer.

So they sat Lauren up in bed and swung her feet over the side. Lauren's head looked wobbly even with her neck brace, and her eye looked far off into an unseen distance. But then her eye focused, and it looked like she caught her balance and her head cleared. They helped Lauren into a wheelchair and pushed her out into the hall where the corridor was straight and easier to follow. They set the brakes on the wheelchair and helped her up. Lauren stood like a soldier.

"Lauren," said the therapist. "I want you to walk, and I want you to walk twenty steps. Do you think you can do that? I've got your arm. Here we go. Twenty steps."

For a moment Lauren stood without moving.

"Come on," I said under my breath. I could see Cheryl and Brittany were praying.

Shakily, Lauren took a step.

"C'mon," I said again. "Twenty steps, Lauren. You can make it."

Lauren took another step and still another. She kept walking. One step after another. We all grinned from ear to ear. Our expectations for her had been far too low.

Suddenly Lauren stopped walking. She didn't move. It was almost like a switch in her mind had flipped and her body had turned itself off.

"What is it, honey?" I asked.

The therapist steadied Lauren.

"Lauren?" Cheryl said. I could hear the alarm rising in her voice.

"Lo, do you need to sit down?" Brittany asked. "Hey—I think she needs to sit down."

"Thirty," Lauren said quietly.

"What do you mean?" the therapist asked.

"Steps," Lauren said.

Thirty steps. In all of our excitement over Lauren walking, we'd lost count. But Lauren hadn't. The therapist had asked for twenty, and Lauren had given ten more. We were beyond ecstatic. It meant that not only was Lauren walking, but her brain was working so well that she could count silently to herself. Caroline wrote about the incident on CaringBridge that day, and it was reported on the news that night. I received texts from all over. One person wrote, "Thirty is my new favorite number."

On Thursday Lauren walked again, this time a little farther. She rested throughout the afternoon, and when she woke up, she was stringing a few sentences together, even talking and laughing. Some words were slurred, and others just didn't make sense. For reasons unknown, she kept calling everybody a "nugget." She would request things in her line of sight, but the words she used wouldn't match the objects she wanted.

Brittany asked her if she had any dreams, and her clear response surprised us all. "I had a dream about big, beautiful flowers," Lauren said. "And in my dream I said, 'Thank you, Lord, for letting me see such beautiful things.'"

The no-visitor policy continued all that day and the next.

On Friday morning Lauren was walking and talking more. She also, however, started talking about pain for the first time. "My fingers just ache," she said. "Dad, you've got to uncurl my fingers."

She was talking about the fingers on the hand she'd lost. I tried to explain that to her.

"No, Dad, no. You've got to do something about my fingers. I can feel them. Please—they hurt so much!" We called the nurse. More pain medication was administered, and Lauren slept.

When Lauren woke up she said that she was hungry. This was the first time she'd said anything like this, and we were all excited. We asked what she was hungry for.

"Sweet potatoes," she murmured. "And maybe some Brussels sprouts."

Her two favorite foods. It wasn't exactly easy to find those two menu items in the hospital, but a while later someone located them, maybe from a store somewhere nearby, I don't know. But when the food was brought to Lauren, she wasn't able to eat. She just slept.

On Friday night Lauren's fingers were hurting again. This time she spoke to Brittany. "Britt—you've got to fix my hand. My fingers are crossed over. Please, you've got to do something."

Brittany kept her voice calm and steady. "Lo, you remember what we talked about. Your hand feels like it's there, but it's not."

Lauren nodded like she remembered, but twenty minutes later she asked the same thing. She tried to touch her hand, the one that wasn't there. You could tell her brain was hoping to make a connection. Brittany calmly explained to her again what had happened. Lauren nodded, but a few minutes later she asked the same question again. They were trying to lessen her pain medication just slightly by then, and this went on repeatedly for the next hour.

It killed me emotionally every time we needed to tell her, and I tried to think of anything I could do to divert her attention. What she needed to do was sleep. Finally I asked, "Lauren, do you remember when you and Brittany were little girls? When I tucked you into bed at night, I'd always sing the same song. Remember the song, Lauren? I could sing it to you again right now. You need to sleep, honey. You want me to sing you the song?"

"No, Dad," was all she said. Lauren looked so confused.

On Saturday, December 10, Lauren woke up and drank some juice. She walked up and down the hall three times with the help of a therapist. It had been exactly one week since the accident. The prayers for the facial nerve had been answered as we'd hoped. Doctors said a successful connection had been made, and Lauren was able to smile and lift both eyebrows on her own.

Lauren's sweet spirit continued to shine through. She regularly talked to all the medical staff now, thanking them repeatedly for taking such good care of her. They loved her for it. One doctor administered the pain medications, and Lauren kept calling him "Dr. Feelgood."

Still, there was a long way to go. We all knew it. Lauren's eye wasn't making any progress at all. We couldn't understand why God didn't seem to be answering that prayer. We so wanted the eye to be saved, but doctors said that if they didn't see some more progress by Wednesday of this upcoming week, they'd need to remove it.

That night Lauren was in a lot of pain. Her shoulder ached. Her chest ached. She kept asking us to uncurl her fingers on the hand that wasn't there. Brittany was our rock through this. Patiently, time and time again, Brittany soothed Lauren and calmed her down, explaining to her that the hand wasn't there anymore. I was so proud of both my daughters.

At about 10:30 p.m., Brittany left to go home with Shaun. Cheryl was sitting on a chair at the foot of Lauren's bed. I was dozing in my chair next to Cheryl.

"Daddy," said Lauren. I could just faintly hear her voice. It was so soft from the bed where she lay.

"Yes, sweetie," I said, rousing myself.

"Will you sing to me tonight?"

"Of course," I said and sat on the edge of her bed. I tucked the blanket underneath her chin and smoothed the hair that still remained on the right side of her forehead.

"Edelweiss, edelweiss . . ." I began softly, the same song I'd sung to my daughters as little girls.

Lauren opened her eye. I kept singing. She shifted her right arm over and tried to feel where her left hand was. She gave me one final confused look for the night, then relaxed and closed her left eye.

I ended the song like I always did with the last line I'd made up, "Bless Brittany and Lauren forever," and when I finished, my daughter was asleep.

CHAPTER 23

The End of Week Two

Cheryl

On Tuesday morning, December 13, Lauren writhed in pain. It just seemed impossible to regulate her pain medication so that she consistently felt okay. She had no appetite and refused to eat. Doctors said this type of stubbornness might happen. The only person Lauren would respond to, interestingly enough, was Shaun. For some reason, he could be a bit firmer with her, and she would be okay with it.

"Look, Lauren," Shaun said, "you've either got to eat, or they'll put the feeding tube back in. What's it going to be?"

"All right, Bosser Cracker," she said before eating a few bites.

The stubbornness was the only display of anything negative in Lauren's personality. Most moments she was upbeat, positive, grateful, even-tempered, and encouraging. Later that morning she asked Caroline to put up her favorite verse on CaringBridge—Isaiah 40:31, about those who hope in the Lord having their strength renewed.

We'd been noticing that in spite of the heavy medications she was on, Lauren was speaking more clearly, and her sentences were becoming more coherent. Every once in a while she still rearranged words, or completely unrelated words would pop out of her mouth. One morning about ten days after the accident, she wanted to put on some deodorant. "Dad, would you put some sneakers under my arms, please," she said. We don't know where she got the word *sneakers* or why it was placed in that sentence. It made us laugh, but it also kept us praying that everything would get sorted out in her mind.

During her second week in the hospital, the no-visitor policy was lifted, and Lauren could see friends again. Chace Crawford was in town from New York to visit his family for Christmas, and he came to see Lauren. Presents started to pour in from around the country. Stuffed animals, CDs, books, homemade crafts. One seventy-five-year-old woman sent a little blanket she had made "to keep Lauren warm." It was so sweet. A little six-year-old boy sent Lauren a stuffed toy owl, which Lauren loved. While lying in bed, she could never find a position for her arm that felt comfortable, and the owl made a perfect fit to prop up her arm.

Parkland is a hospital that shows its age. It's been around for more than one hundred years. In 1963, after he was shot in Dallas, President John F. Kennedy was rushed to Parkland for emergency treatment. The people at Parkland are amazing, and the services they perform are among the best in the nation. But the building itself has sort of a stale atmosphere, which got to us after a while and made it hard for us to feel clean. Because she'd been in bed so long, Lauren's hair had gotten kind of ratty. Caroline, Brittany, and I wanted to give it a good, deep cleaning. Medical staff agreed, as long as Lauren was lying down. Chris Wilson was visiting, and he went out and bought some good-smelling shampoo for Lauren. We ran back and forth from the sink to her bed with cupfuls of water. They gave us a suction hose to vacuum up all the water. Lauren was laughing as we washed her hair. When it was all over, her head smelled fresh and clean—not an antiseptic kind of clean, but just a regular Lauren kind of clean.

I was so happy to see Lauren enjoy that shampoo. We were finally beginning to experience a little sense of normalcy. She also began to mention the magazine, and I was grateful she remembered that *LOLO Mag* existed. Her normal personality shined through in bits and pieces, giving me a sense of relief that the Lo we knew was beginning to emerge again.

At the same time, I felt scared as I wondered how this was all going to turn out. At this point I was just in survival mode . . . putting one foot in front of the other and trying with all I had to be emotionally strong for her and everyone else. My sister eventually took me off to the side and told me to stop worrying about all the people who were visiting. For once, she said, I didn't need to take care of them.

I was numb. Exhausted. Emotionally spent. I didn't know how I was going to make it. Jeff and I hugged a lot but didn't talk much. We communicated through eye contact, and that spoke volumes. We reassured each other of our love and thankfulness that God had restored our marriage and family. Without a doubt, a deep love existed between us.

XO

For the past several days, Lauren had needed to do a lung-clearing breathing exercise with a device called an incentive spirometer, where she would suck air through a tube and, in doing so, raise a blue marker within the device. This procedure helped prevent pneumonia, a common post-surgery complication. Lauren never enjoyed doing it, but she learned to make it into a game to see how long she could hold up the marker by taking strong, deep breaths. One afternoon she took the tube and acted like it was a microphone. Each time she inhaled into it, she said, "Yes, and what is the next question for *LOLO Mag*?" Due to all the medication, we weren't sure if she was consciously making a joke, or if she actually thought she was back conducting an interview for her magazine. We assumed the best. Her performance had me, my sisters, and Jeff's sister laughing so hard we could hardly breathe!

I'm glad there were a few bright moments along the way. It helped us to get through the darker times.

Right after the accident, the cells in Lauren's left eye had begun to knit together, but little progress had been made since then. Because I had held out so much hope for a miraculous healing for her eye, my biggest struggle came when I was told it could not be saved. Early on Wednesday, December 14, doctors removed her eye. No one knew exactly how to process that. It was a bad day for everyone, for sure.

But even then I didn't question God. I consciously reminded myself that I trusted him and that he knew what he was doing. I asked God to increase my faith because, as a mom, I so wished I could take on the pain for Lauren. Why couldn't it have been me? Why didn't I go flying instead? I wanted more than anything to put myself in her place. But I couldn't. I couldn't change a thing. I've always been known as a strong person . . . the oldest of five, very responsible. Yet inside I felt helpless and desperate.

Not only that, but Jeff and I had gotten so little sleep that I was amazed we were able to converse and carry on normal activities. On the outside, I appeared to be in control. Whether because of exhaustion or grief, though, I often felt as if I were having an out-of-body experience or functioning like a zombie.

On the day Lauren's eye was removed, I vacillated between feeling hugely disappointed that the eye wasn't spared, yet hugely thankful that her life had been. Truly, I was so grateful my daughter was alive and making such rapid overall progress. Not only was she beginning to respond to us, she had not come down with a single infection. Considering how many contagions Lauren encountered when running into the dirty propeller blade and then falling onto the runway, that was truly miraculous. Her traumatized body might have been unable to fight an infection, and we might have lost her.

Then there was the eye surgery itself. The doctors had said it could be tricky, yet they reported that it had gone unbelievably well. They put what they call a "placer" into the empty socket and bandaged it up.

When Lauren woke from surgery, she was in a lot of pain. The pain ebbed and flowed the rest of the day around the medications administered. For a while after the surgery, Lauren was lucid and able to talk. She was so sweet, telling me how much she loved me and wanting to hold my hand. Then her pain returned, this time with excruciating force. Once she'd been given the maximum dosage of pain medication, there was nothing we could do except wait it out. I began to pray out loud, the only prayer I could think of just then, "Jesus . . . Jesus . . . Jesus." Then we prayed together, "Jesus, take the pain away. Jesus, take the pain away." We said it over and over again until we both would doze off to sleep. At last more medications were administered. When the pain subsided and she finally dropped off to sleep for the night, Lauren looked so peaceful, almost like an angel.

People talk about a special "twin connection," and over the years we've found that to be true with our daughters. Right after the surgery to remove Lauren's eye, Brittany's left eye started to twitch. Every thirty seconds or so her muscles contracted. This went on around the clock for about two weeks. Then the twitch was gone. Brittany's right eye never twitched, only her left.

XO

On December 16, they moved Lauren to Zale, a different wing of the hospital that had a strong neurosurgery/neurotherapy department. Hospital administrators were concerned about the press, as we were. Mike's friend Clint owns a security company, and he had his team come in to facilitate the move. It was quite a sight to see. The security team had all these huge ex-Special Forces guys on staff, and they mapped out the travel route and lined the hallways. One burly guy put a hat with a floppy brim on Lauren's head, which covered most of her face. The entourage wheeled her to the elevator bank and down to the basement, then rolled her over to Zale, and up and over to her new room. All the time they were communicating through their walkie-talkies and checking around every corner. It was absolutely awesome. You'd have thought the president was on the move.

At Zale they changed Lauren's code name again. Instead of "Lauren Sky," her name was now "Lauren Andronski." I had no idea if it meant something, but Lauren thought it sounded cool, like a name for a secret agent in a movie. The room at Zale was nicer and newer, with a view out the window of downtown Dallas and even a small, adjoining waiting room with a couch and another bathroom.

When that weekend rolled around, I couldn't believe it had already been two weeks since Lauren's accident. That Saturday night, Jeff and I sat silently watching Lauren sleep. We were peaceful, resting in the quiet of the new room at Zale. Jeff reached out and took my hand, and I held it warmly.

"I love our kids so much," I said. "She's going to make it, you know. She's really going to be fine."

Jeff smiled. "I feel the same way. God has big plans for Lauren, and I can't wait to see what they are. We just need to keep taking twelve hours at a time."

"Yeah, but we need to pray for something more. This request's personal to me, Jeff, but I really want it to happen."

"What?"

"I want Lauren home for Christmas."

"That's less than a week away, Cheryl. You mean 'home to visit' on Christmas Day?"

"No. I want Lauren home for good."

"You know the enormity of what it would take for that to happen?"

"I know, Jeff."

"Okay," Jeff said with a smile. "Let's pray."

CHAPTER 24

Christmas

Brittany

We all started to pray that Lauren would come home for Christmas—
and come home for good. We told Lauren about it too. She's always
responded well to a challenge, and we wanted to give her a big goal to
shoot for.

Lauren's appetite returned, and she started eating on her own more
consistently. Each day that week she went through intense physical,
occupational, and cognitive therapy sessions. She began to get up, walk
around, shower on her own, and dress herself in sweats and comfortable,
loose-fitting clothes. It was good to see her wear something other than
hospital gowns, and I think she felt more like herself in her own clothes.
She was even able to ride a stationary bike, which amazed us all.

She wasn't out of the woods by any means. The pain kept coming
and going. Her memory flickered on and off. Her missing hand kept
bothering her. Time and time again she'd forget it was gone and ask one
of us to uncurl her fingers.

But she kept her sense of humor too. One afternoon the maxillofacial surgeon came in to examine her scar up close and see how well her facial nerve was healing. He was a young doctor whom I didn't recognize. He asked Lauren to smile and lift her eyebrows. As the doctor was leaving, I asked him, "Can we have your personal number just in case we need to reach you?" He smiled and gave it to me.

When he left, Lauren said in a hushed tone of mockery, "Brittany—did you just ask that cute doctor for his phone number?" She knew she was being funny.

As Christmas drew nearer, Shaun and I wanted to throw Lauren a little party, just to help us all get in the holiday mood. We decided on a slumber party, just the three of us. We rented the old, corny movie *The Santa Clause* with Tim Allen, rearranged the couch in the adjoining room, and cuddled up on it to watch the movie. It was about as much fun as we could have in a hospital room.

That night while Lauren was in bed, she began to moan in pain. There was always a five- to ten-minute window between the time her pain medications wore off and her new dose was administered. All we could do during that stretch was distract her and pray that the minutes would pass quickly.

Shaun sent me somewhere across the room to get something, then clicked on his iPad and asked Lauren for advice on what Christmas gift he should get me. Some earrings maybe. A necklace. It was such a normal-sounding request, something he would easily have asked his sister-in-law about before the accident. Lauren followed his lead and began to offer her perspective on various gift choices. It bought us time until the nurse came in with the next dose, and Lauren's pain subsided.

I was definitely concerned about all the pain medication pouring into my sister's system. We all were. Lauren's body mass is so slight to begin with, and she was acting so upbeat and positive. In many ways she's like that normally, but now in the hospital she was almost a little too positive at times. Her personality was her own, but it wasn't quite hers, either. Lauren hadn't cried yet at all. She hadn't expressed any grief over the loss of her hand or eye. She hadn't been angry or sad or worried or concerned. I wondered how much of what was truly going on inside her was being masked by the meds.

XO

Mom and Dad kept talking and praying about Lauren coming home for Christmas. I talked and prayed about it too, but maybe I was trying not to let hope rise, just in case Lo wasn't able to leave the hospital. From what the doctors were saying, it sounded like she'd need to be in rehab forever.

On Tuesday, December 20, my mom called my cell phone. I work in accounting for a commercial insurance company and had gone back to work by then, adopting a schedule that allowed me to be with Lauren as much as possible. Each evening after work I'd stay with Lauren until late, then early in the morning I'd go in for a while before heading to work. When I answered my cell phone at my desk that day, I could hear Mom was crying. But it wasn't sad crying.

"They said she could come home," Mom said. "And it's going to be this Friday!"

I couldn't believe it.

On Friday, December 23, we packed up Lauren's hospital room. It felt almost like moving out of an apartment. There were flower arrangements everywhere and cards by the boxful. We packed up two carloads full of flowers and gifts. The doctors discharged Lauren. We bundled her up and, for security's sake, scurried her out the back door to a waiting car.

It had been only three weeks since the accident. Three weeks since the paramedics thought Lauren wasn't going to survive. In that time we'd witnessed a resurrection of sorts. Lauren had been given back to us. How many people had prayed during that time? How many people had hoped? How many people had donated food, written e-mails wishing her well, or sent heartfelt gifts and letters expressing sympathy? How many people had been touched by the miracle of Lauren's recovery? There was still a long way to go, but this was one huge mile marker in the journey. Lauren was coming home for good.

As we thought ahead to Christmas, we were grateful that we had done most of our Christmas shopping early, before December 3. Dana Crawford said not to worry about a thing—she'd finish our shopping for us. We figured she'd just pick up a few extra little items.

Having Lauren home for Christmas was amazing. Someone had given us both these crazy, colorful pajamas with matching socks—bright red with large, white polka dots. Lauren and I put them on and posed for a picture in front of the Christmas tree in Mom and Dad's living room. Shaun texted the picture to family members with the tagline, "Merry Christmas from the twins."

On Christmas Eve, Dad gathered us in the living room and read the Christmas story to us. Just for fun, he also read us a couple of books from our childhood—*The Night before Christmas* and *The Polar Express*. Then we all went to bed. Shaun and I spent the night there, and the whole house felt cozy and peaceful and magical and happy.

On Christmas morning we got up and ate breakfast. At about 10:30, Dana texted my mom, "Santa's ready to come over."

Two cars showed up. Dana and her family had shopped for all of us. They provided a bigger Christmas than we had ever experienced. There must have been forty presents. While Dana and her mom carried in armfuls of gifts, Chris brought in Christmas dinner. We were speechless and humbled. It was one of the greatest examples of what true community should look like, the hands and feet of Jesus caring for other people, even to provide more than they could ever want or need.

The rest of that day was filled with joy, peace, and rest. Lots of friends stopped by throughout the day. We just hung out, watching the Cowboys play on TV, talking, napping, and laughing. That night Lauren slept for thirteen hours straight. She woke up only to take her meds before peacefully going back to sleep.

Lauren was alive. She was functioning almost normally again. She was home from the hospital in record time. It was a Christmas we'd remember forever.

CHAPTER 25

Heavy Weather

Lauren

Everyone in my family would remember that Christmas forever—everyone except me.

I don't remember much of it.

While it may have appeared to other people that I was functioning well, the progression back to full consciousness was much more gradual in my mind. During those weeks in the hospital, I was just so woozy. So in and out of it.

I don't remember walking thirty steps. I don't remember being transferred to Zale. I don't remember going into or coming out of any of the surgeries. I don't remember my dad singing "Edelweiss," although I wish I did.

I can remember a nurse calling me Sky and not knowing why she did it.

I remember getting my hair washed and thinking it was funny because everyone was getting so wet. I remember the moment, but none of the details.

I remember Carol, the nurse we knew from church. She stayed with me one of the first nights after the accident because my parents needed to rest. I remember feeling such peace having someone I knew there. I woke up a couple of times. Carol said she was sleeping, but she jumped up from her bed each time I awoke.

I remember my grandma coming to the hospital, but hardly anyone else.

They say that following an accident, the medication is actually good for you emotionally because it helps lessen the blow after a major trauma. If you hear you've been in a serious accident and you're not on medication, you freak out. I remember very clearly waking up in the hospital and asking my parents why I was there. They told me about the accident, and I remember saying nonchalantly, "Oh, okay." I didn't feel startled by the news at all.

I can remember being home for Christmas, but not leaving the hospital. I remember Christmas morning and that we got those cute pajamas. Brittany and I wore them, and we took a picture. Or maybe the picture was taken on Christmas Eve.

For years I've been writing in a journal nearly every day. The entries stop on November 30, 2011. They begin again on December 29, 2011. In the latter entry, I wrote in nearly the same handwriting as I did before. The entry said matter-of-factly:

> It has been about a month since I have written because I got
> majorly hurt. Such a disaster—I lost my left eye and left hand.
> It is truly devastating, but I want to look above that. God, you
> have a huge plan in this. I believe that with all of my heart, and I
> have already seen parts of it. The story has been all over the *Today
> Show*, *Good Morning America*, etc., and people's lives and faith are
> being greatly affected. Thank you, Lord. Thank you, Jesus. I pray
> that I can heal effectively and quickly. I certainly believe I can
> and will. I can't believe I was already home three weeks later.

There's a sense in which all of that is true. Yet there's a sense in which that's the sanitized version of things. There's no detail included in that entry. No emotion or grief of any depth expressed on the page. The tone is nothing like how I usually write, and much of the entry is the medication talking.

When I came home from the hospital, I was still on seven different types of medication. They started to wean me off them gradually, almost as soon as I got home, but it would be another several weeks before I was completely off them all. As my medications decreased, I began to get a better sense of my situation.

I remember waking up one morning, maybe just before the New Year. I remember sitting on a chair at the kitchen table and feeling so tired. So extremely exhausted. I was almost too tired to sit on a chair. I went back to bed.

I remember my arm hurting almost constantly. The pain could be spiky and thudding, both dull and sharp at the same time. It would curl down from my left forearm, and I'd feel all my fingers still there, cramping and aching. By then I knew in my mind that my fingers weren't actually there. But my body hadn't come to accept it yet. There was no way to lessen this pain. You can't medicate a phantom limb.

XO

It was perhaps the second or third day of the new year, 2012. My pain medications were still being cut down gradually, and I remember I felt more clear-minded this day. The gravity of the situation had been slowly sinking in, and I decided it was time for me to do a little research.

I went into the bathroom by myself, turned on the water of the shower so there'd be cover noise, and locked the door. In that particular bathroom, there's a nearly full-length mirror. I also got a hand mirror, so I could see behind me.

As anybody might do, I stood in front of the mirror without my clothes on, completely vulnerable against my own scrutiny. For the first time since the accident, with my mind more lucid than it had been in weeks, I examined the results of the accident on my body.

On the top of my head, the shaved side, were two different, long scars. The propeller blades must have popped me twice before I jerked away. One scar was horseshoe shaped. It extended from the front of my head to almost behind my ear.

On the left side of my upper forehead, my skull was dented, and the skin over that section dipped down. Titanium plates had been placed underneath the skin to stabilize my skull, since part of my skull had been removed when they did the brain surgery. Despite the plates propping things up, I now had this ridge in the top of my head that extended down to just below my hairline.

One scar ran down the left half of my face—from the top of my forehead through my eyebrow, the edge of my eye socket, and part of my cheek. The scar ended just above my lip. My lip sagged slightly on one side.

My left eye was entirely missing. The upper and lower lids were cut through, and the whole eye socket drooped.

The scar began again behind my left shoulder. It ran up and over my shoulder through my collarbone area, down below my armpit, and through the pectoral muscles of my chest.

My left hand was missing. The wrist bones were gone, and my arm ended just below where the wrist would have been.

Oh, and four teeth were cracked.

I stood looking at myself for at least ten minutes. And then I looked away.

From deep within me a storm of mourning brewed and broke forth. A dark, dangerous funnel cloud seemed to hit the ground. As I climbed into the shower, the storm hit, and the rain fell all around me. I grabbed a shampoo bottle, just trying to move past the grief I was feeling right then, I guess. But I couldn't open it with only one hand. The shampoo bottle fell from my grasp, and I stood for a moment, utterly ruined. Then I crumpled to the floor of the shower and sobbed.

CHAPTER 26

Hope Disguised

Lauren

For some time, the days were dark.

Weeks, even.

There were a few good, unclouded moments—and one or two that were even ablaze with sunshine. Near the end of the first week in January, James visited. He brought me a bunch of stuff for a garden he knew I wanted to plant in the spring. Seeds for tomatoes and cucumbers, spinach, arugula, strawberries, and herbs. Even though we had broken up, I was still glad to see him.

"I'm going to be here as long as you need me," James said. And I knew he meant it in the best possible way. I smiled, and we hugged.

I got a huge lift a few weeks later when I saw a tweet from Giuliana Rancic, whom I'd met briefly during Fashion Week the previous September. "Inspired by you, Lauren Scruggs," she'd written. "You will come out of this stronger w/more meaning to ur life. Your spirit is inspiring. Praying for u :)"

Since Giuliana had recently been treated for breast cancer, her words carried a lot of weight. Not only that, but I'd long admired her passion for her own work, both as an *E! News* anchor and as founder of FabFitFun, a women's health, beauty, and fashion website. Her message left me with one of the first glimmers of hope that I wouldn't need to let go of my goals and dreams, despite my life-altering injuries.

"Thanks so much," I tweeted back to Giuliana. "I really appreciate it. I believe your sweet words. Hope you are doing well too :D."

People reported on our exchange, noting that the two of us had more in common than our careers and health battles: we had both been public about how our faith was helping us through some of the toughest times of our lives.[15]

Though not reported, Robin Roberts from *Good Morning America* also contacted my family not long after the accident. In fact, she e-mailed us several messages of encouragement, using her strong faith and portions of Scripture that she said had helped her during her fight against breast cancer years before. Here was another upbeat, stylish, faith-filled woman encouraging me to keep fighting, to keep moving toward my dreams. And because she had done it herself, her words were truly meaningful. Having an example like hers to follow during my recovery made a difference.

Robin mentioned that through all her challenges with health, she'd always wanted to be treated normally, which I could completely relate to. I was finding that I hated being treated differently because of the loss of a hand and an eye. Being babied or pitied just made me feel worse.

Some of my greatest challenges lay ahead, and I reread Giuliana's and Robin's words often in the weeks to come. They helped me believe a normal life was possible again, which enabled me to hold on to hope. That was so important—because right then, just about everything else in my world felt murky and overcast.

Beginning in early January I'd started going to Baylor's outpatient rehab center five days a week. My parents and I would drag ourselves out of bed each morning. I never knew how I'd feel once I woke up. Often I was sad; sometimes I would begin crying for no reason. More often than not, I was in pain. On a typical day at Baylor's rehab program, I would walk the hallways and toss tennis balls. I also worked with a speech pathologist, did memory tests, and talked with a counselor. On most days, I had two or three doctor's appointments after rehab. When my parents and I got home around 7 p.m., we would find a meal in a cooler that friends had left for us. By that time of the evening, though, I was usually so physically and emotionally exhausted that I went straight to bed.

All the Baylor therapists were kind, but the rehabilitation program wasn't working for me. Most of the other patients in the program were stroke victims. They were all pleasant people, and I found myself wanting to help them out any way I could. But when my dad realized that I was spending most of my time encouraging other patients rather than focusing on my own recovery, he was visibly agitated. "It's fine that you're helping other people," he said. "But right now you're there for *you*—not them." He began researching other options for long-term rehabilitation.

As my medications were continually lessened, sleeping at night became next to impossible. I'd never had a problem sleeping before, but now I twitched throughout the night, tossing and turning. I just could not get comfortable. Mom often slept in my bed to make sure I stayed calm throughout the night. We developed a kind of routine: Dad and Mom would come into my bedroom in the late evening, and we'd all pray together. Then Dad would go back to their bedroom, and Mom would stay with me. She'd pray with me more and then read some Scripture or a devotional. When I fell asleep, she'd still be there, sleeping with one ear tuned in to me like she did when I was a newborn baby.

I was so truly grateful to my family for surrounding me with such love. Each day I seemed to need their care in a different way. Once I'd come home from the hospital, my core temperature seemed impossible to regulate. One minute I burned. The next minute I froze. My arm hurt so badly. It pained me to raise it above rib cage level. It felt awkward and heavy, like a broken tree limb about ready to fall.

My physical and emotional resources felt bankrupt. I was absolutely drained. Some days I'd get up and start making my bed, and then I'd climb back in and roll under the covers into the fetal position. One morning I woke up and went to the kitchen to eat breakfast. As I sat there, I felt like I was going to topple over. I wasn't dizzy, but I couldn't stay awake. That wasn't like me at all.

By January 17, I had been weaned off all my pain medication. That's when depression hit—hard. I felt like I'd been decked with a kickboxer's roundhouse. Mostly I felt low, yet my emotions fluctuated all over the place. I was no longer the generally upbeat girl my family had seen in the hospital—the one who, when I first saw that half my head had been shaved, said, "Oh, that's not so bad." Of course, I'd been drugged out of my mind at the time.

As soon as I was able, I got hair extensions put in. The stylist brought out nine packages of hair but ended up using a total of thirteen. She attached the extensions with tiny metal beads. They were a blessing to have but made my hair feel heavy and unnatural.

Even though I felt more like myself once my hair had been fixed, every time I saw myself in the mirror, I cried. In fact, I avoided looking at myself as much as possible. Losing the eye was hard enough, but losing the hand was something I could barely begin to cope with emotionally. While I reasoned that the missing eye could be covered up, the loss of my hand was so obvious. When it was bandaged, I could hardly look at the end of my arm, much less when the bandages were off. The doctors said that when a limb is amputated, it can feel like losing a family member in the way you grieve and process through it. Sometimes I'd wake up in the morning and think, *Wow, what a horrible nightmare.* But then I'd remember. *No, it wasn't just a dream. My hand really is gone. It isn't something I can ever change or fix.*

XO

Then, suddenly, in marched the anger.

One evening I was sitting on the couch with my parents in the living room. We were watching some mindless TV show—*The Bachelor*, I think, with all these beautiful girls vying for the attention of a single guy. I looked at the end of my bandaged arm and thought, *I'm never going to be that pretty. I'm never going to be normal. I'm ugly. Just ugly.*

From out of nowhere this rage rushed over me. It was absolutely primal, uncontrollable. I started yelling. "My life is ruined! No one will ever love me! I am so ugly!"

My parents jumped up and tried to help me work through my fury. My dad tried to hug me to help calm me down, and I pushed him in the chest—which is almost laughable because he's so big and didn't even budge. But the horrible part was that my mom came closer, and I shoved her, too.

That's not how I am.

Ever.

I ran down the hallway, panicking, crying, still caught in the grip of rage. When I finally exhausted myself, I collapsed on my bed. They say that when someone is hurt, it's common for that person to lash out at whoever is closest to him or her. That's what happened that night. I was so sorry later.

As my parents stood nearby, unsure how to help, I said, almost in a whisper, "Get Brittany over here." It was a demand, not a request. She was the only person I wanted to see. My parents called Brittany, and she and Shaun drove straight over.

As soon as I saw my sister, peace came over me. I can't quite explain it. Being in my twin's presence offered a sense of calm that no one else in my family could provide just then. It was fine that Shaun was there too. In normal times, Shaun is one person who doesn't need to try hard to make me laugh, and when he walked in the door he said something that made me crack up—a long, wild, hysterical laugh. I don't know if what he said was actually funny, or if it was just that my emotions were fluctuating so ferociously. "Shaun, stop it!" I remember saying. "I want to be angry now."

"C'mon, Lo," Brittany said in a firm, quiet voice. "Let's get you into bed."

In the weeks to come, the strange, sudden outbursts of anger happened more than once. This rage was new to me. Once I stormed out of the house after yelling at my mom, all because one little statement pushed me over the edge. I knew I was hurting my parents by this unusual behavior, and that tore up my heart. My dad brought us all together and reminded us that we are a team as a family. We needed to work together and not attack each other. Hearing that perspective helped.

One day I was so angry that I desperately wanted to hit something. Dad had heard me ask every one of my doctors, "Will I be able to box again?" As a result, he had talked to my rehab doctor and neurosurgeon about it. Both said it would be fine as long as I was careful not to allow anything to hit my head. Taking up boxing, they agreed, would be a constructive way for me to channel my anger and grief. Not only that, it would be a sign to me that life could return to normal and that I didn't need to let go of all the activities I loved. So when I told my dad about my pent-up rage that day, he went out and got me a present: a punching bag. It felt so good to hit that bag.

My mom and dad were so wonderful through this. They'd absolutely put their lives on hold to care for me. They didn't blame me for my erratic behavior.

Dad remained a rock of strength for me. He prayed for me every morning and every evening. He read psalms to me, or portions from Isaiah. I often woke up early in the morning—4 a.m. sometimes—and wandered out to the kitchen. There he was, already reading his Bible at the kitchen table while the coffeepot burbled on the counter.

Morning, evening, and throughout each day, Mom took care of me. She read to me, opened bottles of shampoo, helped me get dressed, snapped my jeans shut for me, tied my shoes, helped me do my hair, drove me to appointments, picked me up from appointments, prayed for me, and massaged lavender oil into the end of my arm. "You're beautiful, Lo," she whispered, over and over. "Absolutely beautiful."

One evening Mom and I were lying in my bed. I was hurting badly and rolled over onto my chest to see if that would provide a better position. Mom began praying out loud that God's peace would descend on us in a new and special way. She prayed for a conscious sense of rest in our hearts—even more than that, she prayed that we would feel the serenity of God in the room.

When she stopped praying, it grew utterly quiet. I could hear her breathing next to me. Outside I could hear crickets on the lawn in the Texas nighttime air.

"Lo," Mom said softly. "Are you still awake?"

"Yes."

"What do you feel right now?"

"It's so comforting, Mom. So comforting."

"Can you feel the peace?"

I looked over at my mom. "Yes, and I never want it to end."

We both fell asleep, and when I woke up in the night, my arm was around my mother. The arm with my missing hand. She was asleep too. And I left my arm around her.

CHAPTER 27

Dana's Picnic

Lauren

Although that one good night was a wonderful respite, I continued to have wild mood swings. I battled anger, depression, fear, rage. Some days I felt so utterly low. All I wanted to do was sleep.

One morning I stayed in bed crying. I couldn't get up, and I didn't even want to try. Mom asked repeatedly if she could do anything, but my answer was already no. Finally I asked if she could have Brittany come over again.

Brittany arrived with my best friend, Caroline. I first met Caroline in elementary school, but our friendship really solidified during high school. Ever since then, we've been a part of each other's lives. Now, standing by my bed, Caroline was all business. "Here's the deal, Lo," she said. "We've got to get you out of the house. At least for a while. It's tough enough for any twenty-three-year-old to go through what you went through. But it's also tough for a grown-up to be dependent on her parents all the time like you are right now."

"Caroline's right," Brittany said matter-of-factly. "We're all going out."

I saw the wisdom in what they were saying. Pretty much all I had done for weeks was stay at home and go to therapy. Both these girls knew me well. What I needed was to be pushed forward. To be challenged to climb out of the trap I was in.

It was a simple afternoon out. They drove me to Willow Bend, a mall close to our house. We just walked around and got a snack and coffee. I bought a brightly colored shirt at Forever 21. I wore a baseball cap along with my eye patch and kept my left arm covered by a long sleeve. Because of the hair extensions on the shaved side of my head, my hair looked normal from a distance. Still, I couldn't help worrying that people were looking at me, wondering what was wrong.

It felt good to be out. But when we came home, I was exhausted. I curled up in my dad's favorite chair in the living room and napped.

Day after day, Brittany and Shaun were absolutely wonderful. They recognized that a regular change of scenery was going to be good for me and began to invite me to stay over at their house on weekends. We'd pick up Chinese food and rent a movie, or just hang out and talk. Sometimes friends from my college days would come over, and it felt as normal as anybody could make it.

About the only video game Brittany and I had ever played as kids was Super Mario World. We tried to play it again, but of course I quickly realized you need two hands to work the buttons. Brittany sidled up next to me, and we both played with the same controller—she worked the left side buttons, and I worked the right. The first few times it was hard, but we soon got to be pros. The teamwork was fun too.

One night while I was staying over at Brittany and Shaun's, I began to feel so depressed. Fears and insecurities rolled around in my head. I've never been a jealous person. I've always celebrated Brittany and Shaun's close relationship. My negative thoughts weren't even directly related to them. This was more about me feeling sorry for myself. Alone in the spare room, I started crying, then got myself together and called James. We talked for a bit like we'd always done. Then the waves of depression came over me again, and I started blubbering while we were still on the phone.

"I could have had what they have right now," I said to James. Meaning marriage, a home, a normal life. The lament was directionless, and even I didn't know if I was referring to James specifically or my desire for a normal life in general. Fortunately, he didn't ask, and he helped talk me through my grief that night. I remember him saying, "I'm going to be here for you as long as you need me," and it felt like I'd heard that somewhere before. James was such a good friend. I was so glad he was still in my life.

During those first few weeks back home, I didn't know what goal I was working toward other than to keep pressing forward. As tired as I was, as depressed as I was, as up and down as I was, I just tried to keep moving on. I prayed and read my Bible and went to therapy every day and tried to heal the best I knew how. Back on January 9, I'd written my first blog post since the accident—just a simple message of thanks to everyone who'd poured out their love for our family.

It felt good to write again, even the tiny bit that I wrote that day. But no matter how hard I tried to regain a sense of normalcy, there were still huge questions I couldn't answer and didn't know what to do with. I worried about all the things I was sure I'd never be able to do again. How was I going to water-ski or go rock climbing or box with only one glove? How was I supposed to drive with only one eye? Or dress myself with one hand? Or style my hair, or open a jar of pickles? I was sure no guy would ever think I was attractive again—much less want to marry me.

I worried about my career. How was I supposed to type quickly with only one hand? How was I ever going to blend in at Fashion Week so I could interview models? I couldn't picture myself next to all those beautiful fashion industry insiders. I felt nervous about spring and summer approaching. I didn't want to go outside without long sleeves. I didn't want to be seen in public. The bottom line was that I was never going to be normal again. That's what I told myself. Normalcy, as I'd known it, was long gone. I wanted to lock myself in my bedroom and never come out again.

XO

One morning I woke up and dragged myself to the kitchen. I felt exhausted. So I dragged myself back to bed. Mom had an appointment somewhere, and Dad was at their office, so she needed to leave me all alone.

"I can cancel my appointment, Lo," she said. "Really, you're not going to do anything dangerous are you?"

"I'll be fine," I said into my pillow.

Mom left. I dozed, I think, because the next thing I knew, the doorbell was ringing. From somewhere my brain told me it had rung more than once. I wanted whoever was there to go away. But the bell rang again, so I shuffled to the front door and looked out.

Dana Crawford stood on the front porch. I opened the door and started crying. I cried and cried and couldn't stop. Dana just hugged me and held me. I kept crying, and she did the only thing she could think to do, I guess. She started singing. "You are my sunshine, my only sunshine . . ." The song made me laugh. Not a frantic, erratic, emotional laugh this time. But a relaxed, normal laugh.

She hugged me again. "Why don't you come over to my house today?" she said. "A change of scenery would do you good."

I snuffled and nodded, went back to my room, and threw on some clothes. Dana drove me two streets over to her house. She made us a picnic lunch—a salad with a lot of fresh, crisp vegetables and a tangy herb dressing. It was a sunny day with a refreshing breeze.

"Let's eat outside," she said. "We need to get some vitamin D into your system."

While we ate, Dana asked me what I was thinking. I poured out all my concerns, worries, and fears to her.

"There will always be lies in your head," Dana said. "But let's compare the lies with truth." One by one she listed the facts. I was still alive. I could still think and talk. The accident could have left me brain-dead, but it didn't. People loved me dearly. I was being well provided for. I was going to be able to relearn how to do many of the activities I'd always enjoyed. Guys were still going to find me attractive. I'd still be able to do my job. Ultimately, God was a good God, and he had a plan and a purpose for everything I was going through.

Talking with Dana brought such clarity to my heart and mind. As I sat there, soaking up the wisdom she was giving me, I thought to myself, *You know, I just feel like sitting in the sun right now and not saying a thing more.*

Right then Dana said, "Do you just want to lie back? I'll pray over you."

So I did. I lay back in the sunlight, and Dana began to pray. After that, we sat silently together for maybe half an hour.

That time was so joyful, so peaceful. It was then I realized that I had needed to face the darkness before I could truly see the light.

It was my turning point.

CHAPTER 28

Vacation in the Snow

Lauren

Mom and I were sitting at the kitchen table one afternoon, feeling hopeful about the progress being made, yet still wrestling with feeling overwhelmed by all that was going on. Mom said, "Y'know, we all just need to get out of here for a while."

"I feel the exact same way," I said.

We talked about where we might go. Dad walked into the kitchen and mentioned that family friends, Michael and Debbie, had offered the use of their home in Colorado anytime. When we called, these friends dropped everything they were doing and changed their schedule to accommodate ours. The next weekend Michael and Debbie flew our entire family to Steamboat Springs for four days. It was the first vacation we'd taken as a family since the accident.

Their home was beautiful—like a lodge, yet still homey and cozy. Just the sight of the front door made us begin to relax. Outside it was snowy, with the Rocky Mountains ringing the panorama, and the scent of pine trees in every breath. I felt secluded, sheltered, and at peace.

Shaun and Brittany came, as well as James. It made sense to extend the invitation to him, too. James was a good friend, and he'd been so caring throughout the aftermath of the accident. He got along well with everybody in our family. Plus he loves the snow and the mountains, and I knew it would be fun for him to get away.

We all pretty much took it easy. I did, anyway. The guys went snowboarding and skiing. I wanted to go along, but doctors had told me I couldn't risk a fall. Whenever there's been brain trauma, a person's head is extremely vulnerable for at least a year, even after the wound has healed. So instead of snowboarding, the girls all went into town and got facials.

Each day I felt us unwind more and more. Mornings were spent sleeping in, drinking coffee, making pancakes, eating leisurely breakfasts, and hanging out by the fireplace. Afternoons were filled with walking, drinking more coffee, and having lots of deep, contemplative conversations. We cooked dinner in the evenings and hung out together. One night I went with the guys to the mountain to watch a community celebration called the Night Extravaganza. When darkness had fallen, skiers whizzed down the mountain with torches in their hands. They twisted and turned in long, serpentine arcs, and everyone cheered as the torchlight parade went by. It felt so good to celebrate something again. For the whole weekend, we didn't talk about the accident or rehabilitation much, which was refreshing.

I've had a Twitter account ever since the social media site was invented, and toward the end of that trip I tweeted two photos, as I would have done normally while on vacation. One shot was of me and Britt mugging for the camera. We've got our sunglasses on, and we're making these exaggerated hippie looks, laughing at ourselves. The other photo was of a group of us during the nighttime event in Steamboat Springs. Immediately after I tweeted them, James noticed what I'd been doing and gave a low whistle. "Lo, you can't be serious," he said.

"Why, what's wrong?"

"You know those pictures are going to end up on the *Today Show*, don't you?"

"Oh, sure. That's funny, James."

But as he'd predicted, the next day we got an e-mail from the *Today Show*. The photo of Britt and me was shown on several national media outlets; then it spread to various other media sources along with a story about how I'd taken my first vacation since the accident. I was shocked at the exposure.

"The problem," James said to me, "is that you're still thinking you're living the life you've always lived. But your life is not like that anymore, Lauren. You can't just tweet a picture for fun like you used to."

XO

James was right. For some time I didn't comprehend how large the news story surrounding my accident had become. I'd always been used to going places and not worrying about who was watching. I remember how one afternoon we started getting texts from people saying a picture of me was all over the news. It seems that an unidentified photographer had snapped a photo of my dad and me arriving at Baylor's rehab clinic. The story was all over the Internet, and the caption below the picture in most stories said that we were "all smiles." But that was so wrong. Dad and I had been listening to a worship CD in the car. We were both crying, just trying to work through all our emotions. Normally my dad just dropped me off at rehab, but I was having a tougher day than usual, so he went in with me. In reality, far from being "all smiles," we were both a mess in that picture.

Another photo that made it all over the news showed me leaving Whole Foods with Sharon Kendall, who'd driven me there. Going to stores still felt new to me. Complete strangers would stop us with tears in their eyes, saying they had been praying for my family and me, which was cool. The caption stated that I was leaving a local gym, but that was incorrect.

Another picture was snapped from the street as I came up the walkway in front of our house. I'd just returned from rehab. We never did see who took the pictures, and the photographers never talked to us, but they must have been camped out near our house, just waiting to zoom in their cameras and get a close-up shot. From then on, we were advised to take different routes from the ones we normally drove. It was eerie to think that people were hiding out, trying to take my picture.

Dad sat me down and had a similar talk with me. I'd never actually seen the list of media sources that wanted to do interviews with us, but he showed it to me. It was crazy. All these huge names were on the list—Dr. Phil, Ellen DeGeneres, *People* magazine, the Associated Press, the *Times* in London, the Hallmark Channel, *Cosmo* UK, *Glamour* UK. The list stretched on and on. I was even asked if I'd consider being a contestant on *Dancing with the Stars*.

"Remember the CaringBridge website?" Dad asked. "The one that Caroline and Sharon set up so they could communicate with our friends and with people who wanted to follow the story?"

I'd seen it several times. Sharon had been printing out some of the comments for me that had been posted there. The messages were sweet and gracious. People wished me well and said they were praying for me. No one had said anything about how many hits it had received.

"Look again," Dad said.

We logged on. The site had received more than a million and a half hits. I poured through page after page of comments—thousands of them—left by people from all over the world. Time and time again, people wrote about how my suffering had touched their hearts. They thanked God for our family and said that God was using our experiences to inspire and lift up others who need encouragement.

- "Hello, Beautiful Lauren," read one. "I am a Catholic who has not been as in tune with my church as I should be. You and your mother's writings have inspired me in so many ways. I know your life is different now and measured in increments of good and bad times throughout the day, but knowing that you have a strong belief in the works of the Lord is a blessing. You are strong and will get through this, but please remember that you are beautiful and always will be. Much love to you and your family in this difficult time of healing! xo, Leslie."

- "Your strength is amazing," read another, from a woman named Nancy.

- "I just wanted to let you know how uplifted I am by your journal," read a comment from Mary. "I hope Lauren continues to recover, and that your family continues to live by faith. Please know that there are many, many people who have been touched by your family's story as it unfolds, and continue to pray for you."

- "Lauren, you have shown such grace and dignity thru it all," read another. "Thank you for allowing us to be a part of the daily struggles and successes. Lauren, I don't know you, but I love you dearly, and I know God has a beautiful plan for your life. I will continue to keep you in my prayers."

- "Lauren," read one from Jenny. "Saw you on the news today, and you look AMAZING!!!! I have been following your story and wanted you to know that you are such an inspiration to all! God bless you!"

I was speechless. I hadn't been trying to do anything extraordinary. All I'd done was try to keep moving forward—just like Casey, my friend from high school, had done. Her father had died and her brother had gotten sick, and there were huge moments of pain in her life when all she wanted to do was lie down and quit. But she didn't crumble under the weight of all the hardship that hit her. I'd drawn strength from her example and from watching others who'd gone through adversity.

I'd developed my definition of everyday courage—*Even when life hits you hard, you keep on going*—then lived by that definition.

That's all I'd done.

XO

It felt good to have James on the trip with us. He hugged me a lot, and I hugged him right back. He was so sweet, so protective. At dinner one night I was having problems cutting my chicken. He reached over and cut it up for me, without me even asking.

On the last afternoon of the trip, James and I went snowshoeing, just the two of us. Above us, the Colorado sky was blazing and blue and cold and clear. We hiked a short way out into the woods and came to a clearing where we stopped. We weren't too far away from the lodge, but just far enough so it felt private.

"James?" I asked. "Um . . . are we dating again?"

He looked far away into the mountains and thought for a moment. I wasn't sure how he'd answer. My heart was beating fast, and it was one of those moments when, had we been dating, we would have kissed.

"Lauren, you know I care for you a great deal," he said. "But I don't know if I'm that person to you. I'm here as your friend, not as your boyfriend."

I scuffed my snowshoe along the ground. Somewhere far away I heard a bird flutter to a tree, chirp, and then go silent. "Well," I said, "maybe if you and I were still dating, it wouldn't be such a bad thing."

"Maybe."

"Maybe it would be good. Just like before."

"Maybe," he said again. "Or maybe we still need some time to sort things out."

I nodded. We hugged, a really long hug. He held me so warmly, and I wanted to stay that close to him for a long time.

We both understood the seriousness of a conversation like that. We weren't toying with the idea of dating for dating's sake. We were sorting through an incredibly big decision—whether to reconsider the idea of spending the rest of our lives together.

And James was right. The answer wasn't clear, even though that moment in a snow-covered clearing was perfect. We needed to be genuine to ourselves and to what we knew to be true within the larger context of our lives. We both knew it was too soon after the accident to begin dating again. We needed to live for a while in this "new normal" and give our friendship time to adjust.

Still, in that one moment, everything between James and me felt perfect. I wish it could have gone on forever.

CHAPTER 29

My New Reality

Lauren

Our trip to Steamboat Springs reenergized me. I was going to beat this thing, I decided. Whatever I needed to overcome, I would.

Weeks before, I'd begun going to a prosthetics company in anticipation of eventually getting a prosthetic for my left arm. An occupational therapist there suggested that I check out a new rehabilitation and therapy program at a center called Athletes' Performance. The center specializes in training professional athletes, some of whom have had injuries. It looked more like a gym than a hospital.

Sheri Walters, my main physical therapist there, normally has a tightly packed schedule, but she "just happened" to have an opening when I called. Sheri is a few years older than me and absolutely amazing. We connected instantly. I was in awe of her education, skill, knowledge, and dedication. I quickly realized how much more beneficial it would be for me to do rehab with pro athletes rather than stroke patients. I knew that this was exactly the place I needed to be.

Five days a week I met with Sheri. She started each session by working on my various scars, massaging a special cocoa butter formula into the wounds so they didn't constrict or begin to seize up. Then we worked through various training exercises. She wanted me to do push-ups to strengthen my upper body. I lay flat on a workout table, and she held the end of my left arm for support. When I first began, I could hardly crank out one push-up.

"Don't worry, Lauren," she said. "This is only the beginning."

We worked with weights and running, stretching and lunge work, as well as wraps and compresses to reduce swelling in my residual limb. The whole environment was different from my first rehab center. This time my fellow patients were football players with torn shoulder ligaments, soccer players with knee injuries, and baseball players with twisted back muscles. Some were athletes without any injuries at all—they were simply there to train during the off-season. Rock music boomed from overhead speakers. I gave it my all, and in a short time I could do twelve full push-ups—not from my knees, but full push-ups from my toes. I didn't even call it physical therapy anymore. I called it "training."

Early on I told Sheri about how I'd learned to box before the accident, but that I'd concluded I could no longer participate in the sport. "Actually," she said, "boxing would be helpful to your recovery. The cardio is good, but it will also teach you how to judge depth perception again by hitting a moving target. I'll see what I can do." She wrapped my left arm and fitted me into my pink gloves, then called in Stewart Gill, the center's general manager. He was a huge man who'd been a US National Taekwondo team member for eleven years. Stewart had me do some warm-up drills by alternating my stance. Then we began to spar. I was pleasantly surprised, both by how well the glove held to my left arm and by the fluidity of my movements.

"Nice job, Lauren," Stewart said when the session was over.

It was such a simple phrase of encouragement, but I felt empowered, like I was well on my way. Since then, I've continued to practice taekwondo regularly at the center. It feels so good. Before the accident, I learned how to box because I wanted a new challenge in my workouts. But since the accident, martial arts have helped me heal.

It seems as if I am doing what I had been doing before, but in a new and intense way.

About five weeks after I came home from the hospital, I met with an eye specialist, Randy Trawnik, to be fitted for a prosthetic eye. The procedure is complicated, and it sometimes takes several days to create the eye, color it, and be correctly fitted for it. But Mr. Trawnik brought me in on a Saturday to see if we could do it all in one day. He'd lost an eye himself in the military, and when he came out of the service, he retrained as an ocularist. I could tell instantly he was passionate about his work.

We began in the early morning. Mom, Dad, and Brittany came with me. The whole process was fascinating. First Mr. Trawnik took an impression of my eye socket, which he used to mold a wax model eye. After carving and shaping the wax model, he used that to create the plastic prosthetic eye. Then he hand-painted it and added finishing touches to make sure it looked as realistic as possible. Mr. Trawnik worked in stages. He would keep us in his office for a while as he measured and inspected me, and then he would send us out for an hour or so while he worked. We'd go to Starbucks or wherever and then come back for another step in creating the eye.

Most fascinating to me was watching him paint my eye color. He had a whole palette of colors to choose from. He'd look at my right eye intently with a magnifying glass, then paint a bit on the prosthetic eye, then look closely at me again. I asked him to describe all the colors he saw in my eye. He said my eye is a green-hazel color, mixed with a hint of yellow in the middle, and flecks of blue, gray, green, and a little bit of brown. I loved watching him paint. I've always been captivated by art and color palettes. It reminded me a little of the feeling I get when I have a new set of markers to work with.

When Mr. Trawnik finished painting the eye, he let me hold it. The prosthetic eye feels sort of like a clay bowl that hasn't been hardened in a kiln yet. The surface is firm but pliable, too, almost with a skin feel. The eye is not completely round like a globe, either, but more oval shaped.

To fit the eye in my socket, Mr. Trawnik put drops in the socket and then slid the piece in. At first it felt weird, tight—like something that shouldn't be there—and it looked lower on my face than my other eye. Surgeons had told me earlier that this would happen. They'd need to go back and do another surgery to add volume to the lower part of my left eye socket in order for the prosthetic to look nearly identical to the right eye. Mr. Trawnik shaped it further so it would fit perfectly.

At about 4:30 p.m. I left wearing my new eye. I couldn't believe it. The prosthetic is designed to track with my other eye so they move in sync. Eventually my muscles will form to it and treat it like a regular eye. I can leave the eye in the socket indefinitely. I don't need to take it out to sleep or shower or anything.

My doctor suggested I wear glasses to protect my prosthetic eye, but I'm not always willing to do that. Glasses feel restrictive to me, and I don't like the way I look in them. Besides, how can I box my heart out when I have glasses on? Sometimes, though, I just don't want people seeing my prosthetic eye; I'd rather hide behind my aviator sunglasses.

One reason I'm self-conscious about my prosthetic eye is that it doesn't move as fast as my other eye. Fortunately, Mr. Trawnik referred me to some of his past clients who have learned to compensate for having an artificial eye. For instance, one TV reporter he worked with has learned how to blink naturally. When she's on camera, every time she looks from right to left, she purposely blinks. That way people don't notice any difference in the speed of movement between one eye and the other. I learned that getting a prosthetic involves both the process of fitting the eye and then learning how to use it. Overall, getting a prosthetic eye was a positive, encouraging experience. It left me feeling more whole again.

Getting my prosthetic hand, however, has proven to be a much bigger challenge. The problem stems mostly from the difficulty I have had accepting the idea of a prosthetic limb. To me, losing my eye didn't feel as overt as losing my hand. Even though I hated the loss of sight in one eye, the eye itself could be covered. But a missing hand is much harder to pass off as normal looking.

It initially took four meetings to pick out the new limbs. I was fitted for several prostheses since each would look and function much differently. Also, I didn't know it just then, but after the first four visits

I would need to return to the arm center countless times in the weeks and months to come. Some weeks I'd be there three days in a row and spend up to four hours at each appointment. When you lose a limb, trips to the prosthetics center become a regular part of the rest of your life. You're constantly getting things checked, breaking a part of the artificial limb and having it fixed, or having something refitted or adjusted.

The people at the center were wonderful to work with, yet the visits themselves could be so frustrating and draining. Sometimes it was easy to start feeling suffocated with exhaustion and internal tension. The night after an appointment often proved very difficult, and I'd be either angry or utterly sad afterward. Each time I went to an appointment, I progressed a little further, but the trips were still hard.

At one of our earliest meetings, they showed my mom, my dad, and me various hands and arms. The majority of people who lose limbs are guys, they explained, so all the model arms were male, with hair on them. Honestly, seeing all those arms lying on the table freaked me out. The experience brought back the reality of my situation. I was going to have a fake hand for the rest of my life. At first I wasn't crying. I just felt sort of numb and asked questions quietly. Then I cried. We all did. On the ride home, everybody was emotionally drained and silent. "What did you guys think about today?" I finally asked.

Still crying in the backseat, my mom spoke up. She described having many conflicting emotions, which articulated well how I was feeling too. We were thankful that I could get a prosthetic hand. But the whole experience felt surreal. We couldn't believe this was my new reality.

A meeting soon after went a little better, but not much. The administrators of the hand clinic had asked a woman with only one arm to come in and speak with me. She was sweet, cute, and energetic. The clinic meant the gesture in the best possible way, but I wasn't ready for it yet. It was too much information for me to process that early. The woman took off her prosthetic arm, and I fell apart, crying really hard. She was kind, but I just couldn't handle the thought of me doing that action anytime soon. I kept picturing myself in different situations—trying to wear a sleeveless dress again, what it would be like to go to the beach, what people would say if I went jogging wearing a tank top. I couldn't go there in my mind yet. Not at all. I needed to leave.

Sheri, my physical therapist from Athletes' Performance, came with me the next time. I trust her a lot, and she asked all the right questions. It helped having her there, and this time they made a casting of my arm. I stuck my arm down into a forming mold that looked like a big can filled with gooey material. Once the goo had hardened, I pulled my arm out, and they used the mold to create a plaster cast—similar to the wax mold used to create my prosthetic eye.

Because Sheri helped me get just the right information and asked questions with a positive, matter-of-fact attitude, I was finally able to face some decisions. I opted to get four different types of arms. One is called the "passive." It looks the most realistic, with fingernails and natural skin color. The hand doesn't move at all, but I figured I could use it for professional settings, like going to Fashion Week or attending formal events.

The next arm moves electronically and allows me to hold on to things. It's considered a good, everyday hand. It looks slightly realistic, and it can be used to open a jar or even open a door. The muscles in my forearm make the hand move. By pushing up or down on the muscles, I can make the hand open or close. I got to the point where I could use the sample arm pretty easily.

The last two arms I chose are for recreation. The first is a workout hand/arm that is versatile and can adapt to lots of activities. Different pieces can attach to it, depending on the activity. For instance, it has a clasp at the end that could be used to hold a ski rope. Second, I selected a pink swim sleeve that wraps around my arm like a sock. I felt okay about that.

In addition, we looked at things called "heat gloves" that cover the end of certain prostheses. The gloves protect the hand itself so you don't burn it if you inadvertently pick up a hot pan or accidentally slice it with a steak knife. They warned me that I'd undoubtedly go through three or four of these gloves over the first couple of years. Everybody does.

My new hands were put on order. They would be custom-made, and we were told they would be ready in about six to eight weeks.

XO

In the midst of those difficult and draining appointments, we were invited to a special evening called the LoLo Event, a benefit organized by friends to help cover my medical bills. The event planners told us very little about what to expect—they simply gave us the basics on when and where to go for the fashion show and dinner they were planning.

On March 7, we arrived at Agora Studios, just as we'd been instructed. When we walked into the room and saw 250 people there to support us, we were blown away. The highlight of the evening for me was the fashion show produced by Rhonda Sargent Chambers, whose firm, RSC Show Productions, specializes in fashion show production and event planning. Models from the Campbell Agency walked down a runway made of pink sand. They wore spring fashions from Intermix, Stanley Korshak, VOD, Blinc, and Five Forty Ten. Seven area restaurants provided the dinner while Downtown Fever, an area band, performed. A silent auction was also held.

My parents spoke for our entire family when they thanked everyone and gave some examples of how we'd seen God's power at work. So many people had spent hours volunteering their time to plan this special night, thoughtfully incorporating some of my favorite styles, foods, and music into the event. We were also grateful that the organizers had not allowed press coverage, which made it much easier to relax and mingle with guests all evening long.

Actually, we were still perplexed at the continuing interest in my story, as well as the way the press went about getting photos. In early spring, the paparazzi snapped another picture of me heading over to the store to get some new running shorts. It was a last-minute decision for me, and the picture was taken near the store. The photographer must have been sitting in our neighborhood and followed us there. Probably trying to get a picture of me with my new arm. Too bad for them the arms were all still on order.

I didn't lose any sleep over it.

CHAPTER 30

A Big Misunderstanding

Lauren

Something else, though, was beginning to keep me up late at night. It was a question I needed to settle.

Plain and simple, this question had to do with my responsibilities. Specifically, how much money did I owe?

Dad had been highly protective of me regarding any information about the financial repercussions of the accident, and he'd been taking care of all my finances for me since then. Still, I was an adult, and I knew this was my burden as much as his.

I've talked with people who live in other countries about health care systems, and it can be really confusing to explain America's health care arrangement if you don't live here. (Actually, it can be really confusing if you live here too.) The long and short of it is that if you live in America and you're in an accident, your insurance company will pay some of the bill, but not all of it.

Right after college I'd transferred from my parents' medical insurance plan and purchased a policy of my own. The policy I'd purchased was what any normal, healthy, young person would buy—a policy that has higher deductibles, percentages, and co-pays, since I seldom got sick and rarely went to the doctor. With the particular policy I got, however, it meant that the portion of money I owed for any medical bills was going to be fairly high.

"Dad, level with me here," I said one morning at the kitchen table. "I need to know."

Dad let out a huge sigh, nodded silently, then disappeared into the back room, his shoulders slumped. After a bit he came out carrying this huge file, just stacks and stacks of paper.

There were three things to know, Dad explained, and the news wasn't good.

When it came to the medical bills themselves, all the bills hadn't come in yet, and all the calculations of percentages hadn't been divided and added up. So he didn't have a total figure for me yet. But he assured me it was going to be a lot.

Second, Dad had been told that whenever a person has a disability, the cost of living goes up for that person for the rest of his or her life. The extra costs are for things such as increased insurance premiums, new parts for prosthetic limbs, expenses associated with ongoing therapies and for additional surgeries, and innovations and medical procedures as they're invented. The list goes on and on.

The third bit of tough news was *subrogation*, a word I'd never heard before. (Dad said until recently he hadn't either.) *Subrogation* meant that even if I did receive an insurance settlement, my medical insurance company still had a legal right to take a large part of any potential settlement to cover its own costs. Subrogation wasn't an "if" thing, either. Subrogation proceedings had already begun.

I couldn't quite get my head around how much I owed and would owe—both now and for the rest of my life. The financial picture was such a big blow.

But it got worse.

A week or two later, Dad picked me up after training at Athletes' Performance. I slid into the car seat next to him. He backed out of the parking space, then shifted forward and headed out onto the street toward home. "I don't want you to look online today," Dad said abruptly, as if his mind had been on other things.

It was too late. I'd already logged in to my Twitter account and begun to read the postings there. My jaw dropped.

I couldn't believe what people were saying. Horrible, angry things. There was strong profanity laced through many of the comments—and all aimed at me. I'd never seen anything like it.

"Dad?" My voice faltered. "What's going on? What have I done wrong?"

"It has nothing to do with you, honey. You haven't done anything wrong."

I quickly typed my name into a search engine and learned where the comments sprang from. Various headlines reported that I had snubbed a $200,000 settlement offer.

I gulped. This was the first I'd heard of any of this. I hadn't snubbed any settlement that I'd heard of. "Dad," I asked, "what does this all mean?"

"It's a big misunderstanding, Lauren. Unfortunately, people who know only part of the story are taking it out on you."

What had happened was that one of the insurance companies involved had taken an initial position that it was only obligated to pay $200,000—that's where the figure in the news stories came from.

I could understand how at first glance this would seem like a lot of money to people, and why they would think I was wrong to turn the money down, if that had indeed been the case. It seemed like a lot of money to me, too. (Though in reality, compared to what we owed, that amount wasn't going to put much of a dent in the bills coming our way.)

The insurance company had arrived at the $200,000 figure through a technical definition in the policy—that's what was under dispute. Our attorney had filed a legal motion (called a Declaratory Judgment Action), asking a judge to interpret the language of the policy. The attorney needed to file this motion in court, and when that happened, news sources had picked up on the story.

Fortunately, the PR company sent out a correction later that day explaining the situation. I hadn't snubbed any settlement at all. It had all been part of the normal negotiation process that occurs when an accident takes place. We ended up resolving the insurance dispute quickly and out of court.

The morning after the correction was sent out, most news sources set the record straight.[16] But one article appeared along with a picture of me taken completely out of context. The headline read, "Nothing Makes Me Smile Like a Settlement Check."[17]

Sheesh.

The whole experience left a bad taste in my mouth. It was an indication that we were still going through some deep waters, even as we were sorting out the process of continuing on with our lives.

About two weeks later, I went to church on Saturday night along with my mom and dad. When the sermon ends, we usually sing three worship songs before the night is over. That night as we sang the first song, I was deep in thought about everything that had been happening lately. During the second song the room began to get blurry. My real eye grew hot, and I began to cry. We were all standing as we sang, and I reached over and put my arm around my mom's waist and leaned into her shoulder. During the third song we stood like that and both cried.

The third song was "Restoration," the one Michael Bleecker had sung over me in the hospital.

When the song ended, the service was dismissed, and people began to file out of the auditorium.

"Let's just sit here for a while and pray," Mom said.

I nodded, and we sat for maybe half an hour. Mom prayed so boldly, and Dad prayed too, the two of them asking for God's help with every aspect of what we were still going through.

In the middle of the prayers, I opened my eyes for a minute. Down the row from us was a young couple with a blonde-haired toddler. The child was so cute, and she bobbled around patting the seat backs and grinning at everyone. I grinned at her in return. She was so innocent, so unaware yet of the hostilities of life—things far worse even than what had happened to me. A passionate desire for protection rose up within me and focused on her. I hoped she could stay sweet and untouched by life's harshness for a long, long time.

Michael Bleecker finished onstage and walked over to us. He prayed with us, then reminded us of how far we'd come. Back when he'd sung "Restoration" to me in the hospital, my only movement had been to slightly raise one foot. We'd covered many miles on this journey since then.

It helped put things into perspective, even though we still had a long way to go.

XO

There was another specific challenge I wanted to overcome. I thought about it on the drive home from church that night. It seemed like such a small thing, but I hadn't been able to do it since the accident. What I needed to do formed a barrier in my mind, and I struggled to put it into words, even to myself.

People had asked me if the scars on my face and shoulder bothered me, particularly since I work in the fashion industry. The scars did bother me—but mostly because I didn't feel like my normal self. But it wasn't like I woke up every morning by then thinking about my scars. More troubling than my scars was my missing eye, due to loss of sight and the challenges that presented. But the worst aspect of my injuries was the loss of my hand. Part of it was simply the frustration of trying to relearn how to do everyday activities one-handed, plus my ongoing fear that I might never be able to do certain things again. But the other part of my concern was aesthetic. The loss of my hand looked so obvious to everyone who saw me.

I concluded that perhaps the thing I needed to do was mostly symbolic, because this one thing meant more to me than the simple act of wearing a certain article of clothing. The weather was getting warmer. Spring was here—and when spring comes, a young woman's thoughts turn to fashion.

For me that meant it was time to wear short sleeves in public.

That was the challenge.

Such a small challenge, compared with all the greater problems in the world. Such a little thing. Wearing short sleeves in a place where I'd be seen. And yet I simply could not do it. I just couldn't go there. I hated the thought of being defeated. I needed to move forward.

But I didn't know how I could.

CHAPTER 31

Restoration

Lauren

"The challenge is greater than wearing short sleeves in public," Sheri explained to me one morning during training. "The challenge is about overcoming your newfound insecurities that have been caused by the accident. And, actually, that's pretty huge."

"I don't know why this is so hard," I said. "Soldiers are dying in Afghanistan right now, and I'm too chicken to do this one little thing. It feels stupid to me."

"It's not stupid. It might not be a life-threatening problem for you. But it's important to you because it's causing you concern. That means it's something you need to overcome."

"What am I so afraid of anyway?"

"You're afraid that people will look at you and think bad things about you. You're afraid they'll laugh and point. And maybe a few people will have negative responses. But that's their own business, not yours."

I thought for a few minutes. Sheri was right. In the last several weeks she'd become much more to me than my physical therapist.

She'd become a close friend. And she helped me see that this was my new reality. I didn't have a left hand. I couldn't hide that fact for the rest of my life.

So I chose to fight my fear head-on. I chose to run the Katy Trail.

The Katy Trail is a running and biking path that leads into downtown Dallas. It represents Dallas at its best and meanders along creeks and parkways. It's also public—lots of people are always on the trail. The plan was simply for me to run the trail and afterward go to a nearby café for lunch while wearing my same sleeveless workout clothes.

A pretty basic plan, but it represented more in my mind. From this moment on, I wasn't going to hide. I would still wear my prosthetic hand when it arrived—the passive one that looked like a real hand—but deep down I wasn't going to be ashamed of my disability. That's what this challenge meant to me.

I picked my outfit carefully: a bright green tank top with black pants past my knees. My shoes were black with bright green laces.

Sheri came with me for the run, along with an athletic trainer named Sarah. The run itself was simple. We went for two miles, and plenty of people were out that morning. No one was looking at my arm during the run. I quickly forgot about myself and concentrated on my breathing, my pace, and the beautiful day around us.

After the run we went to Company Café, and Brittany and Shaun met us there. I felt a bit insecure at first, because now we weren't running on the trail, and I was sitting there with my arm out in the open. But everyone got to talking pretty soon, and I forgot about how huge the moment had seemed in my mind. James came to the café too. He'd seen me in the hospital right after the accident with my head half-shaved and my face all puffy, but he hadn't seen my arm. It had always been covered with a long-sleeved shirt or jacket. James pulled up a chair, gave me a hug, and ordered lunch along with everybody else. He wasn't fazed at all.

The paparazzi snapped a photo of me that day. The headline began, "Lauren Scruggs Steps Out for First Time Proudly Displaying Her Amputated Limb."[18]

Oh well. I didn't do it for the news. I did it for me.

XO

Although the physical pain in my left arm eventually subsided, the emotional pain never seemed to let up. To help me work through my feelings, in early spring I began meeting regularly with a counselor, and I continue to meet with her once a week.

My counselor encourages me to speak openly about my struggles and fears, and then she consistently leads me to God's perspective on my challenges. She helps me fight the lies I tell myself (and sometimes hear from others) by filling me with the truth. When I try to gloss over my pain, she challenges me to dig deeper into my heart so I can uncover the source of my emotions and find true healing. One of the most important things she's done is help me come to terms with losing my hand.

I leave every appointment at Advanced Arm Dynamics—which generally lasts about four hours—absolutely exhausted. I appreciate the skill and honesty of the people at the arm prosthetics center, who have been open with me from the beginning about some of the challenges of learning to live with a prosthesis—particularly the myoelectric, the one I'd be able to open and close using my forearm muscles. For instance, people who haven't learned to use the arm correctly have been known to inadvertently crush things like computer screens and phones with it. That, and the fear that my new arm wouldn't look or feel feminine, frightened me early on.

When at last my myoelectric arm was ready in late May, my mom, Brittany, and Sheri went with me to have it put on for the first time. I was determined to be strong and calm when they brought it out. Brittany and my mom started tearing up and left the room as it was being put on, but I got through it, grateful I had managed to look "okay" in front of everyone.

My facade crumbled as soon as I got back home. I left the bag with my new prosthesis hidden in the trunk of my car and crawled into bed. Although I'm a morning person who typically pops out of bed by seven or eight, I stayed in bed the next day until early afternoon. I cried and cried, depressed and dismayed at the thought of using this new arm.

For two days, I refused to even show it to my dad. I couldn't stand the thought of looking at it again.

Sheri had asked me to bring it to training on Monday, but I just couldn't. I left it at home. Sheri didn't scold me, but she did insist on driving home with me while I got it. Once back at the center, Sheri took me into an empty room and had me put the prosthesis on. Through my tears, I confessed how afraid I was of hurting someone with the arm, even if I was just giving that person a hug. Sheri "hugged it out" with me just to prove that was untrue. She told me she didn't even feel the arm. In that moment, I had to face the fact that my own fears and insecurities had led me to worry unnecessarily, and I was so grateful to Sheri for challenging me to test my false assumptions against the truth.

Before long, I realized another source of my anger—my "new" hand. I had learned to live without my left hand; in fact, I had figured out how to do most everyday tasks without it. Now I faced the challenge of relearning how to do everything with a prosthesis. In that way, something I was told would make things easier actually seemed to be making life more difficult again.

Thanks in large part to Sheri, who refused to let me wallow in my fear, I learned to operate the myoelectric arm comfortably within just a couple of weeks. I could even hold something as fragile as an egg without being afraid I'd break it.

When I told Dana that I'd gotten my myoelectric arm, she asked me to come over so she could see it. I still didn't feel comfortable wearing it in public, so I walked over to her house without it on. When she met me at the front door, I was crying hard. Dana immediately took me in her arms and prayed with me. What finally dried my tears was the story she told me next. Years ago, Dana said, when she was learning how to play the flute, whenever she'd hit a bad note while practicing in her bedroom, she'd get so frustrated she'd hit the flute against the mattress on her bed. As she told me the story, Dana did an impression of how she'd pound the flute against the mattress. She had me laughing so hard. Then she told me she thought I was mad at the arm, just as she'd been angry at the flute.

She nailed it. I was directing my grief over losing my hand toward this high-tech piece of plastic and steel.

Several weeks later when I was at Athletes' Performance, Stewart, my taekwondo trainer, came in the room where Sheri and I were working. I was wearing my myoelectric arm. He asked if I minded him being there. I shook my head no.

"You know, Lo," he said, "we all face tests in our lives, but that is exactly what makes each of us unique, interesting, and influential." Then he kindly challenged me to embrace where I was at that moment and be confident in it.

Steve, a performance coach there, reinforced this encouragement a few weeks later. "You're doing more than anyone thought you'd be capable of doing," he said. Then he listed off the activities—push-ups, side planks, TRX intervals, taekwondo, and even half marathon training—that I'd been engaged in. He said I needed to acknowledge and own that progress.

In fact, I accepted my other prosthetic arms far more easily because each one served a purpose. Even though my passive arm couldn't move at all, I liked having the option of wearing something that looked so much like a real arm. I knew it would help me blend in at Fashion Week and other industry events. I thought I'd hate my workout swim arm because it looks so much like a machine. But the day I went to pick it up, I got a pleasant surprise. The designers at Advanced Arm Dynamics had studied *LOLO Magazine* to see what the current color trends are and then designed this arm specially for me. It's pink and green—two of my favorite colors. Designing it with me in mind was such a thoughtful gesture, and besides that, this arm doesn't pretend to be more than it actually is. It is a machine, it looks like a machine, and that's okay. Not only that, but it enables me to work out—something fun that I love doing.

Later, Sheri and I came up with nicknames for my actual arms. Tipping the hat to Brad Pitt and Angelina Jolie, we call my left arm "Angie" because it is smaller now than my right arm. The right arm is called "Brad" because it is more buff. We also have names for each of the prosthetic arms. We call my passive arm, the one that matches the finest details of my right hand, "Beauty." My workout arm is called "Beast" or "Pushy" because it can only do pushing moves. The workout swim arm is called "Squirt." And the myoelectric?

In honor of Dana's music lessons, it's "the Flute."

CHAPTER 32

Giving Thanks

Lauren

Weeks passed, and from the outside, life appeared almost normal again.

I was still surprised at how a wave of grief could come over me, even when I was convinced I'd finally found my way into calmer waters. Sometimes this was triggered by a reminder about my loss. As strange as it may sound, sometimes when I look in the mirror, I am still shocked to see I have a fake eye or a missing hand. I also have to fight a new fear: What will happen if I lose my other eye or hurt my right hand?

Yet I value my independence more than ever. I think that's why I sometimes lash out at my parents when I feel as if they are babying me or trying to do for me what I can do for myself. "Just let me struggle and learn how to do it in my own way," I say.

Getting back my driver's license was huge for me. While I had some great conversations with my friends and family as they drove me around, depending on them to drive me everywhere had made me feel like I was fourteen again. I longed for the fully capable, independent lifestyle I'd had before the accident.

Because not all driver facilities conduct evaluation tests, I had to wait awhile to take it. My name went on a waiting list, and I spent a week practicing parallel parking with my dad.

Finally, the day of the test came. Just as I got into the car, we heard reports of some tornadoes hitting our area, and the test was canceled. I was back there first thing the next morning, though, and I got my license.

XO

On a Wednesday morning in late spring, just an average day in my new post-accident life, I got up early, feeling refreshed, and made breakfast for my parents. Holding the pan with my right hand and steadying it with my left arm, I started with pancakes. Then I cut up some fruit for smoothies and whipped it all up in a blender. When I was done, I washed the dishes.

I dressed myself in gym clothes, tied my shoelaces with one hand, and drove myself over to the center for training.

At the training center, Sheri put me through all the regular rehabilitation exercises. Then I threw around a football with one of the quarterbacks who frequents the center. I was able to both throw a spiral and catch the football with ease. This was a big encouragement to me, as I hadn't been sure if I was capable of this anymore.

Some of the guys there were talking trash to me (in a funny way), so we planned a "dance off." I pulled on my sweatshirt jacket, put my hood up, slipped on my aviators, and danced to "Yeah" by Usher. They were cracking up. The staff danced along with me. I talked to a few of the guys at the center, guys I'd met just a few weeks earlier, and caught a rumor that a couple of them wanted to ask me out. What was cool in my mind was to experience a public expression of attraction like that. Guys still wanted to date me—and, I had to admit, that felt good. Particularly now that James and I had reached a decision.

Since we weren't sure our relationship would be the right one for either of us in the long run, we had agreed not to date each other anymore. From Brooks, I'd realized the danger of dating someone who doesn't hold my faith and values. James, on the other hand, shares my faith and has been absolutely amazing through everything. Yet as much as I enjoyed being with him, I realized I was not ready to commit myself fully to him.

Once I was clear on that, I knew I had to trust God rather than give in to my insecurities, which fill me with self-doubt and fear about what lies ahead. Eventually, James and I came to see that we'd been confusing affection with love. We agreed we are better friends broken up than we are when we're in a relationship together. We care for each other deeply, and maybe that affection will turn into something more someday. But for the time being, there are too many unanswered questions for us to keep dating.

I'm not seeking the perfect guy anymore. I know he doesn't exist, and that's where grace will need to come into the relationship—time and time again. It is reassuring to think that God knows who I'm supposed to be with, and when the time is right, God will let both me and the guy know.

I came home from the center, showered, and changed. I was able to open shampoo bottles, put on my own deodorant, and blow-dry and style my hair. By now my own hair had grown out almost three inches, so my hairstylist had removed the old extensions and put in new ones that glued on. They felt so much better, almost like natural hair again. I figured it would take about two years for my hair to grow out fully to the length it was before. But no matter for now.

I'd always loved doing my hair and round-brushing it, which I still wasn't able to do, although I was figuring out ways around that. (I've got a system worked out where the blow-dryer is attached to a fixed stand.) A girl's hair is important to her, especially when she has long hair and it takes years to grow it out. I smiled wryly, thinking about how far I'd come.

As I continued getting ready, I reflected on all the attention given to my story. Before the accident, few people in the public eye knew who I was. After the accident, it seemed like every move I made showed up in a magazine, news story, or online. Life changed so fast for me—in so many ways—and I was still coming to grips with that.

When I was a child, I was always the shy one. Going to New York was a big confidence-builder for me, and I really became my own person there. Developing that stronger sense of confidence as a young adult has helped me today. Still, it has taken a long while to start thinking of myself as a public person. Some days I want the public notice to go away. I just want to be normal again, and I don't want to be recognized whenever I leave the house. Yet I truly have been humbled by people's caring comments and words of encouragement. I also see how God has put this new trait of "being recognized" in my life for a greater purpose.

XO

As I finished applying my makeup, my mind leaped to the plan for today. It had nothing to do with my career or guys or being independent or the fashion world or interviewing anybody famous.

It was simply to deliver some special treats to some special people.

Months earlier, when I was nearly at my lowest, a class of very precious third graders at Prestonwood Elementary School had decided to raise money for me. I'd graduated from the high school portion of the school, so I already had ties there. But I was so surprised and honored by this kind gesture. These little kids had done odd jobs and raked leaves and washed dishes for their parents, and I'd been able to go to the school so they could present me with their hard-earned donation. I hadn't felt too good at the time, but the children were so sweet. They made me brightly colored cards and gave me hugs and told me they were cheering me on.

Today I would return to the school and say thanks.

I drove over to Prestonwood, and Brittany, Mom, and Dad met me there. The teacher announced I was coming, and the kids all smiled and shouted when I walked in.

I'd baked them cupcakes, so we passed those out. The kids all thought they were great. After we'd eaten, the teacher held a question-and-answer time. At first, the kids were all pretty shy. But then they began to open up more and ask things like, "Does your arm hurt?" and "How much can you see anymore?" and "Was it hard for you to go out in public for the first time without your jacket on?"

When the formal class session was over and I was just about to leave, the kids gave me hugs again. Several kids lingered around me in a semi-circle, asking a few last questions. The kids in this smaller bunch held nothing back. They asked questions with the sort of absolute bluntness that can come only from eight-year-olds.

"Um, Lauren," said one boy. "What does it look like?"

"My arm?"

"Yeah."

I could see a number of other students in the semicircle had the same thought. "Well . . ." I tried to formulate in my mind how to articulate what it looked like, but then I switched gears and said in a mischievous, low voice, "You guys want to see it?"

The group of students nodded as one.

I unwrapped my arm and showed them. The kids oohed and aahed. This was part of the ongoing healing process for me. I realized that people will always have questions for me about the accident and my injuries. I can't hide what's happened, and it dawned on me that I'm actually glad when people don't hide their questions either. I'd prefer that people ask so we can talk freely, rather than see them act squeamish or uncomfortable, or pretend that nothing's different. It was a good moment for me—a really good moment. I think it was a good moment for the students, too. They were learning that people don't all come in the same package—and that that's okay.

The little boy who had first asked to see my arm summed up the moment beautifully. He put his hand lightly on my shoulder and gave a relaxed chuckle.

"You know, Lauren," he said, "it isn't creepy at all."

I never could have imagined how the straightforward honesty of a sweet third grader would become part of my larger healing process in such a big way. One simple phrase from him helped transform how I thought about myself. The boy's words—something so small—grew into something big. His words helped heal my grief and helped trans-form my life's purpose, and I reminded myself of his words over and over in the days to come.

After the accident happened, it had been easy for me to believe so many lies. Snippets of untruths floated through my mind and became exaggerated, filling me with anxiety. *My life is ruined. I am ugly. I will never be loved.*

But the truth is luminous. Truth fills me with hope, even when I can't see the future, even when I don't know how my life will all turn out.

Before the accident I'd had my share of insecurities, like we all do. I had been concerned about how to attract guys, and that had led me to become competitive and even make wrong choices about who I dated. After the accident, it was like my insecurities had become a magnifying glass that I turned on myself and my outward appearance, even more than before.

In one utterly traumatic and unplanned moment, my life had been forever changed by a sixteenth of an inch of steel. It was such a small catalyst that almost destroyed my life. And yet a small thing could also change it again for good.

I saw that if I chose to let the accident ruin me, it would. But I was deciding to make the accident work for me. I came to see how there was so much more to my life than being worried about how I looked. With new resolve, I wanted to do something different with my life. I wanted to serve God in new ways, give to others with new depth, and help people more than ever be inspired to live out loud. This little third grader—his coolness, his honesty, his acceptance—gave me fresh courage to keep going in this new direction.

XO

My accident has led me to ask—and hopefully begin to answer—one final question: how can my life be used for something bigger than me? When Joshua first told me that I would be a warrior someday, I just didn't see it. And for the most part, I still don't feel it. But something Sheri told me after a grueling therapy session one day has stuck with me: "Despite some moments of weakness—which obviously are completely normal—you have been a warrior."

Maybe my mistake had been assuming that warriors are fearless, tough, and unbeatable. I've come to realize that warriors aren't invincible; they're just strengthened and energized by hope. For a while after the accident, I lost hope. But slowly, I've come to see the truth in something I heard at church the night of the accident: "You are hardwired for hope. . . . You're always attaching the hope of your heart to something."

I now know that my appearance, guys, and professional success don't provide lasting security. If I place all my hope in them, I'm bound to be disappointed. Christ alone will never fail me; in fact, in many ways, my recovery has been truly miraculous.

That's not to say I'm any less passionate about my work. In fact, Shannon and I launched a refreshed version of *LOLO Magazine* in September that focuses on the topics of fashion, food, and fitness. After studying which elements of the site were viewed most often, we decided to concentrate our coverage on those areas.

God is also opening doors so that I can begin to speak publicly to people about my experiences. In particular, I am passionate about encouraging young girls to put their hope in Christ, rather than in their appearances. Most of all, I want to be a living testimony to the truth that suffering may strip a lot from you and me, but it doesn't need to steal our hope.

Epilogue

The Scruggs Family

It's been an incredible year for our family.

Incredibly difficult, and yet incredibly good.

People wonder how we can say that—how, looking back, we can say in all honesty that the year has actually been *good*. And in some ways the larger answer is something we're still forming within ourselves and working to articulate, although we already know deep down it's true.

Of course, the undeniably best part is that Lauren has been fully returned to us. There's seldom a moment that passes when we don't remind ourselves that she so easily could have died or never been the same again. She sustained major injuries to her brain, left eye, face, left arm, and clavicle. Her doctors continue to be amazed by her progress, and we are convinced that her healing is completely miraculous.

The fantastic news is that today she's still who she always was to us. She's "still LoLo."

Yet there's no doubt we continue to grapple with deep emotional pain. Adjusting to our new normal isn't always bad, however; sometimes it forces us to lighten up. Adjusting to her prosthetic arms, as you know, hasn't always been easy for Lauren. Just a few weeks after getting her new workout arm, Lo put it on for a sparring session with Stewart. As they were bobbing and weaving, she didn't notice that her left arm was sweating under her prosthesis. As she did a roundhouse kick, her workout arm flew halfway across the turf. After a moment of stunned silence, the two of them cracked up.

Our emotions tend to surprise us like that. We can be up one moment and then sucker punched the next by another wave of grief or sadness. At such times, Jeff often opens his Bible and reads the words of David, the Jewish shepherd boy and warrior who was pursued for over a decade by an insanely jealous king. Out of his own dark experience, David wrote: "I sought the LORD, and he answered me and delivered me from all my fears. . . . The LORD is near to the brokenhearted and saves the crushed in spirit" (Psalm 34:4, 18). That is the truth we choose to hang on to when our feelings threaten to drag us down into despair.

We've also found that when we are open and honest about the struggles we go through, it can be an encouragement to others—and they will be open and honest and encourage us in return. Bernie is a young man Lauren met at the arm prosthetics center. He's a few years older than Lauren and lost his hand a few years back. They can totally relate to each other because they've experienced all the same emotions. He's been a great encouragement. Tom is Lauren's age and lost his hand wakeboarding. He and Lauren e-mailed back and forth for a while, grateful to be able to talk with someone who's been through the same thing.

Bethany Hamilton has also been an inspiration to our family. Shortly after leaving the hospital, Lauren watched *Soul Surfer* for the first time, the movie about how at age thirteen Bethany lost her arm to a shark while surfing. We don't know many people who would have gotten back in the water following a shark attack, but Bethany did. Today she's a professional surfer.

A few months after Lauren had seen the movie, Bethany and her mom contacted us just to say hello, and she and Lauren have talked several times since via Skype. It's been more than eight years since Bethany's accident, and she's learned a lot of practical things about dealing with life since then. Even little things. Once, while she and Lauren were on Skype, Bethany put her hair back in a ponytail with her one arm. Lauren asked how she could do that, and right then, Bethany gave her a lesson. The two texted and e-mailed back and forth, and they finally met in person for the first time in early June 2012. Bethany's genuine joy and the way she has faced her fears and returned to the sport she loves have influenced Lauren immeasurably.

At the same time, we never want to minimize the genuine pain that accompanies hard times—the pain we've been through (and are still going through—it's not over yet) and the suffering that so many others experience. Pain is pain. It can be stark and agonizing, and it's never welcomed. One thing we've learned this year is how to identify in new and real ways with people experiencing pain. We are so desperately aware that we're not the only ones who've gone through something traumatic, and there are a lot of people throughout the world who have experienced far worse things than we have.

Lauren's story is just one among so many others that could be written. This book is dedicated not only to the people who have supported us, but to the greater community of people worldwide who are hurting and caring for those who are hurting, to people everywhere who are struggling with missing limbs and missing eyes, to everyday heroes who fight to keep going forward.

Without a doubt we can say that what has brought us through this time of suffering has been our faith. We could not have made it through this year without Jesus Christ as our rock and anchor. One of the questions we consistently get asked is "Why?" If there's a God and he loves us, why would he allow this to happen?

Do we have an answer for this?

No.

We have textbook answers maybe. That God does indeed love everybody, and yet he allows some bad things to happen for reasons only he knows.

In all honesty, though, we still don't know why God in his sovereignty allowed Lauren to experience this accident, and we may never know for certain. But we trust in God's goodness anyway. We walk by faith, not sight, and someday everything is going to make sense. But for this one day, today, all we know to do is trust in God.

Paul David Tripp, the author and pastor who spoke at our church the night of Lauren's accident, has helped us gain a better perspective through his book *Forever*. He points out that when times are good, it's easy to avoid the hard questions:

> We all ask questions, and we all search for answers. At times,
> not knowing and not understanding doesn't bother us because
> we are locked in our busy schedules, distracted by the details of
> life or thankful that our life is comfortable at the moment.

That's where Lauren and our family were at the beginning of December 2011. *LOLO Magazine* was taking off; Jeff and Cheryl had a thriving ministry; and Shaun and Brittany were happily settling down into married life.

Then in an instant, everything changed—including our outlook on pain. "At other times," Tripp writes, "not knowing is painful and scary because we are facing something we can't ignore but are unable to make sense of."[19]

That's how we felt after the accident happened. Tripp continues:

> When you see things around you as permanent, they take on
> too much importance and increase your sense of loss when they
> are taken away. If you mistakenly think that life is only about
> who has the biggest pile of possessions and pleasures in the
> here and now—if you have eternity amnesia—then suffering
> becomes all the more painful and seems all the more unfair.[20]

Exactly. As we battled our fears and watched Lauren undergo unrelenting pain, we came face-to-face with our utter powerlessness and the sense that God is often hard to find in the darkness. And yet, somehow, in the midst of our stumbling and groping and groaning, we finally realized that God had never been absent—he had been there all along, offering us a living hope and a perspective that is much wider than this present life. As Tripp points out, "Because of Christ's amazing grace and his presence . . . we are never . . . left to live inside the boundaries of our own resources."[21]

We've realized how easy it is to view pain as only a negative thing. We tend to think life should go as we have personally planned it. Yet strength forms in the midst of suffering and battle. The seventeenth-century theologian François Fénelon said, "If you push the cross away, your circumstances will become twice as hard to bear. In the long run, the pain of resisting the cross is harder to live with than the cross itself."

Chris Crawford reminded us recently that his most successful and fun days in life have seldom helped to grow his character. But the times of deep pain and struggle have grown him extensively. In that sense, even the days that feel so difficult can be gifts.

What's one thing we hope Lauren's story shows?

Simply that people can grow through adversity. Hardship is part of life. We all experience it to one degree or another. Yet hardship doesn't need to break us. Particularly when we trust in God, who sees the over-arching plan for our lives. We trust that somehow each experience we go through will mysteriously—and sometimes only ultimately—work together for good.

In the meantime, we try to live each day with healthy doses of love and laughter, which seem to get us through the most awkward of times. Not long ago Cheryl and Lauren flew into Corpus Christi to meet Bethany Hamilton, who had invited them to attend her speaking engagement there. Cheryl and Lauren first met Bethany and her mom, Cheri, over lunch. They assumed that after their meal, Bethany would want to leave to prepare for her talk that night. Instead, Bethany and her mom told them they planned to spend the whole day with them—including a trip to the nail salon.

Cheryl and Lauren were so grateful to talk to another mother and daughter who *knew* where they were, who could rejoice that Lauren's life had been spared while understanding the stages of grief and pain our family is still walking through. In the midst of all the serious conversation, there was plenty of laughter, too.

When they arrived back in Dallas the following evening, Cheryl and Lauren were reinvigorated. Life felt almost normal again. As they dragged their luggage behind them through the airport, they passed a coffee shop. They decided to stop and pick up some drinks to enjoy on their ride home. Cheryl ordered while Lauren went to the restroom.

Cheryl smiled at the barista as she set their steaming cups of coffee on the counter. Then Cheryl glanced at their pile of bags and purses. Her heart sank.

As often happens when Cheryl is reminded of Lauren's injuries, her mind went back to the moments just after the accident when she first saw Lauren lying on the tarmac, not yet knowing whether she was even alive. It hit her once again how completely their lives had changed.

Yet this time, Cheryl remembered the courage and wisdom she'd seen in Bethany the day before. *Lauren's life isn't over*, she thought. *This is just our new normal.*

"Lo," Cheryl said, as Lauren walked back to her, "we've got a bit of an issue. How are you and I ever going to carry these bags to our car now that we've got these coffees, too? Know where we might be able to find an extra hand?"

Cheryl and Lauren stood there silently for a minute, looking from their luggage to their coffee cups to each other. Suddenly they both let out belly laughs. Cheryl couldn't stop smiling as she went back to the counter to ask for a cardboard drink carrier. A few minutes later they were on their way to the parking garage. From there they would head straight to Brittany and Shaun's house, where our whole family would celebrate Father's Day together over dinner.

It's true that the accident changed some things forever. Life for our family isn't the same. But it isn't over, either—not by a long shot.

Acknowledgments

This is the crux of the story: the outpouring of pure love, sincere service, and indescribable comfort we have experienced since December 3, 2011.

First and foremost, we want to praise our Lord and Savior, Jesus Christ. We are thankful beyond words for God's protection and provision.

We want to thank everyone who, at the beginning, offered themselves in ways we didn't know about—and still don't.

We want to express our immense gratefulness to all of you who went out of your way to strengthen us. The gospel came alive through your service.

All of you are a revealing of God's love. It was through this beauty amidst the trial that we experienced our ideal of biblical community. We always knew its significance, but now we have seen its pure reality.

We were falling apart, and friends were there to catch us. We didn't even realize where we were going to slip, and people placed themselves in front of us to keep us from falling.

Fellowship came alive like we have never seen before. What a transparent time when everyone generously used their distinct gifts of leadership, wisdom, business, discernment, and mercy to step in, instilling peace over us amidst our helplessness.

These words from the song "Never Once," written by Jason Ingram, Matt Redman, and Tim Wanstall, represent our hearts of gratitude: Scars and struggles on the way, but with joy our hearts can say. . . . Never once did we ever walk alone.[22]

We struggled writing the acknowledgements because there are so many people to thank, and we don't want to miss anyone. We want to thank:

The "first responders" to the accident
The CareFlite team

All those at the accident site who were not first responders or part of the CareFlite crew

The pastors, friends, and community at our home church, the Village Church, who not only prayed but came to the hospital the night of the accident

The staff and friends at Prestonwood Baptist Church

The staff and friends at Bent Tree Bible Fellowship

Other communities at local churches

People and churches all over the world who joined in praying for us and serving us

The teams of doctors and all involved at Parkland Memorial Hospital and Zale Lipshy University Hospital

The entire team at Tyndale House Publishers

Our collaborator, Marcus Brotherton, and our researcher, Matthew Weeda

Greg Johnson from WordServe Literary

A. Larry Ross Communications

Our extended family

All of our friends

Close friends who stood in the gap and took over all the different aspects of our lives

All those that brought meals for over ten weeks

Those friends who coordinated the meals

All those who prayed and are still praying

All those who sent cards and gifts

All those who sent other types of correspondence: phone calls; e-mails; and Facebook, Twitter, and CaringBridge messages

The CaringBridge ministry

All those we know and don't know who planned fundraisers and blood drives

Those still walking closely with us

Baylor Institute of Rehabilitation

Athletes' Performance for their physical therapy and training

Advanced Arm Dynamics

Dallas Eye Prosthetics

Our counselors

Brittany's and Shaun's workplaces, for their flexibility and encouragement

The Hope Center in Plano, Texas

The people who kept Lauren's professional life going when she wasn't
able to

People who went out of their way to make us feel like we weren't alone

Bethany Hamilton for her sweet influence and involvement

The third grade class from Prestonwood Christian Academy

Those restaurants and businesses that supported us immensely

We also thank all of you who are standing with us as we discover our new norm. We often sit around reminiscing with gratefulness over the love that was and is consistently being poured out on our family. We are overwhelmingly humbled.

Endnotes

1 Paul David Tripp, "Advent—Part 2: Awaiting an Advent" (message, The Village Church, Flower Mound, TX, December 3 and 4, 2011), http://www.thevillagechurch.net/sermon/awaiting-an-advent.

2 See Luke 12:48.

3 CNN, "Get Ready for Reruns: Writers Hit the Picket Lines," November 5, 2007, http://www.cnn.com/2007/SHOWBIZ/TV/11/05/writers.strike/index.html.

4 "Ann Demeulemeester Fall 2011: Black Mythology," *FashionWindows*, http://www.fashionwindows.net/2011/03/ann-demeulemeester-fall-2011-2/.

5 The plane is 271 inches long; see http://www.aviataircraft.com/hspecs.html. A 2013 Ford Taurus is 203 inches long; see "2013 Taurus: Taurus Detailed Comparison," Ford Motor Company, http://www.ford.com/cars/taurus/compare/.

6 Sandra Wright, "Some Significant Wildlife Strikes to Civil Aircraft in the United States, January 1990–May 2012," US Department of Agriculture, http://www.faa.gov/airports/airport_safety/wildlife/resources/media/sig_strikes_1990_2012.pdf.

7 The "prop to person" terminology was brought to our attention by the Federal Aviation Administration; see W. E. Collins, "A Review of Civil Aviation Propeller-to-Person Accidents: 1980–1989," *Aviation Medicine Reports*, January 1993, http://www.faa.gov/data_research/research/med_humanfacs/oamtechreports/1990s/1993/9302/.

8 Information was gleaned via private inquiry to the National Transportation Safety Board. Documents were titled: "Prop to person accidents 1982 –1991.pdf" and "Prop to person accidents 1992–2011.pdf." Page numbers correspond to NTSB prop-to-person accidents (for the plane prop accounts only): 1990: 191, 197, 207, 209, 211, 215, 217, 221; 1992: 1, 3, 5, 11, 13, 15, 17, 19, 21, 23, 25, 27, 29, 31, 33, 35, 37, 39, 41, 43, 45, 47, 49, 51, 53, 55, 57, 61, 63, 65, 67, 69, 71, 73, 75, 77, 79, 81, 85, 91, 93, 95, 97, 99, 103, 105, 107, 111, 113, 115; 2000: 119, 121, 127, 129, 131, 135, 139, 141, 143, 145, 147, 149, 153, 155, 157, 161, 163, 165, 167, 169, 171, 177, 183, 185, 189, 191, 193, 195, 197, 201; 2011: 203 (L. Scruggs' accident).

9 John Huggan, "Jack Newton: Whole Again," *Golf Digest*, June 2008, http://www.golfdigest.com/magazine/2008-06/newtonqa.

10 The statistic of idle speed came via an e-mail from a test pilot for Aviat Aircraft.

11 "Lauren Scruggs Accident: 'Didn't Expect Her to Survive,' Takes First Steps," *International*

Business Times, December 8, 2011, http://www.ibtimes.com/articles/263892/20111208/lauren-scruggs-accident-survive-steps.htm.

12 See http://www.neuroskills.com/brain-injury/frontal-lobes.php.

13 See http://today.msnbc.msn.com/id/45565884/ns/today-today_people/#.T48ZHI4t3OE.

14 See http://abcnews.go.com/US/lauren-scruggs-tragedy-parents-speak-models-propeller-accident/story?id=15093570#.T48ZdY4t3OE.

15 Rennie Dyball, "Lauren Scruggs Gets Support from Giuliana Rancic," *People*, January 19, 2012, http://www.people.com/people/article/0,,20562995,00.html.

16 See, for instance, Robert Wilonsky, "Lauren Scruggs and Insurance Company Say They Have 'Resolved the Issues' That Led Model Injured by Propeller to Dallas County Courthouse," *Dallas Morning News*, March 27, 2012, http://thescoopblog.dallasnews.com/2012/03/lauren-scruggs-and-insurance-c.html.

17 http://www.tmz.com/2012/03/31/lauren-scruggs-all-smiles-after-airplane-propeller-settlement/.

18 Article by Rachel Quigley, *MailOnline.com*, April 2, 2012, http://www.dailymail.co.uk/news/article-2124129/Lauren-Scruggs-steps-time-proudly-displaying-amputated-limb.html.

19 Paul David Tripp, *Forever: Why You Can't Live Without It* (Grand Rapids: Zondervan, 2011), 5.

20 Ibid., 95.

21 Ibid., 92.

22 Jason Ingram, Matt Redman, and Tim Wanstall, "Never Once," EMI Christian Music Group Publishing, 2011.

About the Lookbook

Lauren would like to thank the individuals and organizations that helped bring to life her vision for the fashion lookbook:

Photographer
Stephen Vosloo

Wardrobe Provided By
Studio Services at Bloomingdale's
59th Street, NYC
(212) 705-3673

Activewear Provided By
adidas

Accessories Provided By
Lacey Ryan
LaceyClaceyryan.com
www.laceyryan.com

Stylist
Esther Pak
www.estherpak.com

Hairstylist
Toni Brakatselos
(516) 987-6124
TBhairNY@yahoo.com
www.TBhairNY.com

Makeup Artist
Diana Cappolla
(516) 319-3712
DCapp82@gmail.com
www.makeupbydianany.com

Art Direction
Dean H. Renninger
Stephen Vosloo

First Assistant to the Photographer
Russ Heller
(917) 428-8456
russ@russhellerphoto.com
www.russhellerphoto.com

Production Assistance
Nancy Clausen
Barbara Hill

About the Authors
and Collaborative Writer

LAUREN SCRUGGS is a fashion journalist and the founder and editor-in-chief of *LOLO Magazine,* an online lifestyle experience magazine that integrates the food, fashion, beauty, health, and travel industries.

In addition to her work at the magazine, Lauren has served as a contributing editor at *MyItThings.com*, *SMUStyle*, and *PR Couture*. Her work has been featured in numerous online publications.

A 2009 Dallas Baptist University graduate, Lauren has worked in the Michael Kors showroom and reported from New York, Paris, and Montreal Fashion Weeks. She was an intern in the fashion department of the television series *Gossip Girl*. See her magazine at www.lolomag.com.

JEFF AND CHERYL SCRUGGS are authors, speakers, and counselors. Their writings include the widely used book *I Do Again*, which chronicles their thirty-year story of marriage, betrayal, infidelity, divorce, emotional damage and scarring, forgiveness, restoration, trust, and remarriage to each other.

Jeff and Cheryl are the founders of Hope Matters Marriage Ministries in Dallas. They speak at conferences and weekend worship services in churches across the nation, sharing their love story of hope, redemption, restoration, and God taking hold of their lives. See their website: www.hopeformarriages.com.

BRITTANY (SCRUGGS) MORGAN is Lauren's fraternal twin. She works in accounting for a commercial insurance company and is married to her best friend, Shaun.

MARCUS BROTHERTON is a journalist and professional writer known internationally for his literary collaborations with high-profile public figures, humanitarians, inspirational leaders, and military personnel. He has authored or coauthored more than twenty-five books, including the *New York Times* bestseller *We Who Are Alive and Remain*, with twenty of the last surviving Band of Brothers. See his website: www.marcusbrotherton.com.

lolo MAGAZINE

LOLO Magazine is the ultimate lifestyle experience—your one-stop site for industry buzz, fashion reviews, local shopping hot spots, fitness insights, fresh new recipes, and all-the-rage beauty products. At *LOLO Magazine*, living is more than just dreaming—so get inspired to bring your own dreams to life!

Visit www.lolomag.com to let *LOLO* bring life-style to you.

Loving Christ. Loving each other.

Hope Matters Marriage Ministries

Authors, speakers, and counselors Jeff and Cheryl Scruggs are intimately familiar with the sting, heartbreak, and pain from a divorce—and the deep-rooted hope and joy of a fully restored marriage centered on God. Through one-on-one counseling and speaking engagements with audiences nationwide, they passionately seek to share God's heart for relationships and help make marriages whole in his power.

Visit **hopeformarriages.com** for more information.

CP0611

Photograph © 2008 by Trey Hill.

Online Discussion *guide*

TAKE *your* TYNDALE READING EXPERIENCE *to the* NEXT LEVEL

A FREE discussion guide for this book is available at bookclubhub.net, perfect for sparking conversations in your book group or for digging deeper into the text on your own.

www.bookclubhub.net

You'll also find free discussion guides for other Tyndale books, e-newsletters, e-mail devotionals, virtual book tours, and more!